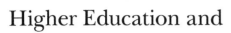Higher Education and

Also available from Continuum

The Consumer Experience or Higher Education, Deirdre McArdle-Clinton
The Future of Higher Education, Les Bell, Howard Stevenson and
   Michael Neary
Internationalizing the University, Yvonne Turner and Sue Robson
Pedagogy and the University, Monica McLean

Higher Education and the Public Good
Imagining the University

Jon Nixon

continuum

Continuum International Publishing Group

The Tower Building	80 Maiden Lane
11 York Road	Suite 704
London SE1 7NX	New York NY 10038

www.continuumbooks.com

First published 2011
Paperback edition first published 2012

British Library Cataloguing-in-Publication Data
A catalogue record for this book is available from the British Library.

ISBN: 978-0-8264-3743-3 (hardcover)
    978-1-4411-6491-9 (paperback)

Library of Congress Cataloging-in-Publication Data
Nixon, Jon.
Higher education and the public good : imagining the university /
Jon Nixon.
   p. cm.
Includes bibliographical references and index.
ISBN 978-0-8264-3743-3 (hardcover)
1. Education, Higher–Philosophy. 2. Universities and colleges.
3. Common good. 4. Community life. I. Title.

LB2322.2.N59 2011
370'.015–dc22

                       2010010987

Typeset by Newgen Imaging Systems Pvt Ltd, Chennai, India
Printed and bound in Great Britain

In memoriam
Ernald C. Nixon
1915–2010

Contents

Preface

It is essential to see the whole garden as an irreducible entity. Everything is con-
nected to everything else.

(Monty Don, The Complete Gardener, *2009)*

A recurring metaphor throughout this book is that of flourishing – and, as
Monty Don reminds us, a place of flourishing must be treated as an irreducible whole in which everything is connected to everything else. If that
is true of gardens and their husbandry, it is also true of the places committed to human flourishing and their stewardship. Higher education is one
such place. Unfortunately, however, unlike the organic garden that Monty
Don has tended for the past twenty years, higher education has endured
innumerable landlords and sitting tenants over the same period. Few have
tended their patch with the care and attention it deserves. Certainly none
has seen higher education as an irreducible whole in which everything is
connected to everything else. Mostly they have been concerned with ensuring that it at least pays its way and if at all possible makes a small profit on
the side.

The belief that there is something intrinsically good and worthwhile
about higher education regardless of its extrinsic goods and costs is central to my work in this area. In my previously published *Towards the Virtuous
University* (Nixon, 2008a) I was primarily concerned with what I called 'the
moral bases of academic practice' and with the institutional conditions
necessary for academic practitioners to flourish as teachers and scholars
(the 'virtuous university' of the book's title). This present book focuses
more generally on the processes of higher education as these relate to
what I term 'the public good' – a good, that is, which in the jargon of
the economists is both non-rivalled and non-excludable. While the ethical
orientation remains much the same, *Higher Education and the Public Good* is
less exclusively concerned with the specific goods of academic practice and

more generally concerned with the relation between higher education and the good of society as a whole.

Although published in 2008, the previous book was written prior to the financial crisis of 2007 and the deepening of that crisis throughout 2008. This book has been written in the aftermath of that crisis, which as it intensified was variously interpreted not only as an economic crisis but also as a moral and social crisis. It seriously threatened the social cohesion of supposedly advanced states that had hitherto been seen as relatively stable and settled; it challenged the market-driven consumerism of the years prior to the economic downturn; and, crucially, it highlighted the extent to which global markets had been largely unregulated, unaccountable, and wholly lacking in transparency. As the crisis unfolded the chronic erosion and diminution of the public sphere was starkly revealed. What Sennett (1977), in a path-breaking book published more than thirty years ago, termed 'the public problem' came back into sharp relief.

For all those with a commitment to higher education the pressing questions related to how and in what form higher education might survive: what, for example, would happen to the 'widening participation' agenda? What would happen to the institutional diversification of the higher education sector and the commitment to differentiated provision? Hard on the heels of these questions followed the equally pressing questions regarding how higher education might contribute to the re-construction and re-invigoration of a public sphere: what, for example, are the public goods of higher education? What are the qualities and dispositions necessary to engage with, participate in, and help shape the public sphere?

The impulse to write this book originated in the felt urgency of these questions. What was clear from the outset was that the implications of the economic crisis and its aftermath need to be fully confronted before there can be any hope of moving forward with a renewed sense of possibility. Chapter 1 sets about that task. If, as I argue in the opening chapter, the financial crisis highlighted the chronic decline of the public good as both an idea and an ideal, then the second task is to re-imagine it for the changed social, civic and global circumstances of the twenty-first century. This task is undertaken in Chapters 2–4. If, however, the public good as imagined in these chapters is ever to be realized, its resources must be located and gathered. Chapters 5–7 set about this task with specific reference to the human goods of higher education: capability, reason and purposefulness. Chapter 8 returns to some of the broader themes introduced in the opening chapter, and by way of conclusion focuses on the challenges and opportunities facing the higher education sector and those institutions that comprise that sector.

The idea of the public good needs to be clearly distinguished from the idea of public interest. Public interest is the aggregate of individual interests or preferences, calculated to maximize human happiness according to the Benthamite formula of the greatest happiness of the greatest number; the public good, on the other hand, involves complex moral and political judgements regarding what constitutes the good for the polity as a whole. What might be calculated to be in the public interest may not be judged by everyone to be a public good. Thus, for example, public broadcasting outlets justify on the basis of public interest the screening of programmes that are judged by many as not contributing to the public good or even as contributing to the erosion of the public good. Whether there is such a thing as the public good and, if so, what constitutes the public good are highly contestable and hotly contested issues.

Equally contestable – and contested – is the question of who is in a position to judge what is and is not a public good. Indeed, the idea of the public good lays itself wide open to the charge of elitism, snobbery, paternalism, etc.: 'who are you to tell me what I should be watching?'; 'I'll watch whatever I want, thank you very much!'; 'Don't you tell me what I can and cannot watch!' This is the recurring strain of those who collapse the public good into public interest and public interest into public preference. According to this refrain, the public good can be read off from the consumer choices of a market niche within the population as a whole. If enough of us want to buy into it and consume it, it is deemed to be an incontrovertible good. That is the logic of a market-driven consumer society.

Higher education – which is, admittedly, itself implicated in that logic – has an important part to play in reclaiming the notion of the public good: first, it provides a dedicated space within which to debate what constitutes the public good; second, it supports the development of an educated public with the capabilities and dispositions necessary to contribute to that debate; and, third, by fulfilling these two obligations it might be seen as a public good in its own right. The purpose of this book is to argue that case. The public good as imagined in the following pages necessarily includes the goods of cultural, economic, personal and social well being, but transforms these into a common resource. Without a fair and equitable system of higher education, this transformation is unsustainable – if not unthinkable. Higher education should be both a manifestation of the public good and the means by which the idea of the public good and its implications for cultural, economic, personal and social well being are conceptualized and actualized through a process of reasoning together.

The purpose of this book is not, therefore, to offer a set of programmatic prescriptions for pedagogical innovation, to specify a set of procedural principles for the systemic reform of higher education, or to provide a blueprint for the structural reorganization of those institutions comprising the higher education sector. No doubt these topics require urgent consideration and no doubt implications can be drawn from the following chapters that have a bearing on these topics. However, this book is both more modest in scope and more tentative in its aspirations. It takes the form of a series of thematically connected essays that speak back to one another as the argument develops. The aim is to reinstate the notion of the public good within the current debate on the ends and purposes of higher education. This task gains added urgency from the restrictive terms within which that debate is conducted: terms that are prescribed by the managerial fixation on bureaucratic efficiency and measurable outcomes. It is the unremitting determinism of the prevailing outlook that requires a renewed sense of possibility.

One of the consequences of this prevailing outlook is that general readerships have collapsed into niche markets. In the field of education these niche markets have become increasingly specialized and increasingly professionalized – a subject I have written on elsewhere (Nixon, 1999; Nixon and Wellington, 2005). It should be emphasized, therefore, that while this book is written with professional academics in mind, it is written neither exclusively for this group nor from within it. Indeed, it is highly critical of the higher education sector as a whole, of institutions of higher education in particular, and of many of the professional and managerial assumptions underlying the practice of higher education. In writing the book I have tried to remain true to my own political colours and intellectual affiliations which place me firmly on the independent and secular liberal left in relation to many of the issues discussed in the forthcoming pages.

Finally, I should emphasize that in focusing on the public good I am not denying the importance of the private and the intimate. The broadening and deepening of the public good enables us to flourish in all aspects of our lives and relationships – including the quality of, and our capacity for, intimacy. The relation between the public and the private is rarely as clear cut as we would like to think. The boundaries are constantly being negotiated and renegotiated with old routines of courtesy becoming obsolete or quant and with new routines emerging within the context of changing social values and expectations. What this book argues is that higher education is a public good, not because it colonizes our private worlds, but because it provides us with the goods necessary to become full and rounded human beings in every aspect of our lives.

Acknowledgements

Many people have supported me directly and indirectly while I have been writing this book. I have, in particular, greatly valued and benefitted from my discussions with Ansgar Allen, Jennifer Creek, Geoff Elliott, Marian Fitzmaurice, John Galvin, Daniel O'Neill and Lesley Rollason and my ongoing collaborative work with Bob Adamson, Feng Su and Jerry Wellington. I am grateful to Feng Su for the friendship and the good talk, Ronald Barnett for the ongoing support and encouragement, and Fred Inglis for providing an exemplar of the socially engaged public educator. My extended family have, as always, been hugely supportive in countless ways: Ben, Hannah and Isaac Nixon, Judith and Neil Ashman, Jessica and Jonathan Robinson, and Amy Robinson and Kofi Broadhurst. Finally thanks to Pauline Nixon for providing the presence – loving and thoughtful – that makes reflective endeavour and explorative talk possible.

Chapter 1

The Public in Retreat

Amid the uncertainties currently facing universities, the only certain thing is that these are all problems which will be exacerbated rather than solved by placing them in the lap of the market.

(Collini, 2003, 9)

The financial crisis of 2007–2008 and its continuing global aftermath have proved Collini right. The economic theories that encouraged blind trust in the providence of market forces have been demolished by events. As Lanchester (2010, xv), in his analysis of the financial crisis, puts it: 'after decades in which the ideology of the western world was personally and economically individualistic we've suddenly been hit by a crisis which shows in the starkest terms that whether we like it or not – and there are large parts of it that you would have to be crazy to like – we're all in this together'. The crisis, in other words, reminds us that individualism is part of the problem, not part of the solution and that whatever solution is to be found will begin with the rediscovery of shared responsibility.

What was lost in the three decades prior to the global crisis was the old and hard-won idea of a public good: a good that, being more than the aggregate of individual interests, denotes a common commitment to social justice and equality. If the collapse of the global markets has done nothing else, it has at least brought back onto the agenda the need to re-imagine the public good, to gather the resources to rebuild a common commitment to the public good, and to define the conditions necessary for that imaginative task of reconstruction. Higher education is central to that task, not only because it is a public good in itself, but because it exists to ask what constitutes the public good. But we start where we are: with a failure of ideas, with the denial of escalating inequality, with a cult of privatization, and with the shameful collusion of higher education in this sorry mess. That is where we start. Because only by starting here – where we are – can we gain a sense of possibility.

A Failure of Ideas

Any great failure should force us to rethink fundamental ideas. The present economic crisis is a great failure of the market system . . . But the crisis also represents a moral failure: that of a system built on money values. At the heart of the moral failure is the worship of money for its own sake, rather than as a way of to achieve the 'good life'.

(Skidelsky, 2009, 168–169)

In the generation following 1945 the gap between rich and poor, whether measured by income or assets, shrank dramatically across Europe and in the USA. By the late 1970s, however, inequality was once again becoming an issue in Western society. 'With the coming to power of Margaret Thatcher and Ronald Reagan in 1979 and 1980 respectively,' writes Skidelsky (2009, 101–102),

markets were deregulated, taxes were lowered, trade unions were bashed, and the international institutions were emasculated. The Bretton Woods philosophy of managed global capitalism was replaced by the Washington Consensus – a term coined . . . to denote the neoliberal policies advocated for developing countries by the US administration: free trade, privatization, deregulation, balanced budgets, inflation targeting , floating exchange rates . . . Free markets would deliver *better* results than fettered ones. (original emphasis)

The ensuing two decades saw the ascendancy of the 'new right', the rise of neo-liberalism as the dominant economic orthodoxy and a new consensus on the need for a 'rolling back' of the state. These were the Thatcher-Reagan-Blair-Bush years of tax and employment 'reforms' and the deregulation of the financial sector: policies which ushered in a prolonged period during which the gap between rich and poor steadily widened – and is still widening – and the dream of instant wealth became part of a bubble mentality. They were the years that at the time seemed to some to be the end of history but that in retrospect emerge from the dust and the racket as an inglorious interregnum: 'never in the history of finance has the market for dreams of instant wealth been so massively accommodated. The dependence of the whole rickety structure on continually rising house prices was rarely made explicit' (Skidelsky, 2009, 7–8).

Skidelsky (2009) is, at the time of writing (December, 2009), the best guide to the collapse of that 'rickety structure'. (Lanchester, 2010 and Stiglitz, 2010, also provide superb analyses, but were published rather later.) The story of the collapse starts with 'a global inverted pyramid of household and bank debt . . . built on a narrow range of underlying assets – American house prices'. It continues: 'when they started to fall, the debt balloon started to deflate, at first slowly, ultimately with devastating speed. Many of the bank loans had been made to "sub-prime" mortgage borrowers – borrowers with poor prospects of repayment'. The denouement is predictable: 'securities based on sub-prime debt entered the balance sheets of banks all round the world. When the houses started to fall, the banks suddenly found these securities falling in value; fearing insolvency, with their investments impaired by an unknown amount, they stopped lending to each other and to their customers' (Skidelsky, 2009, 4). This caused a 'credit crunch', the banks to fail, stock markets to fall, and the economy to slide – at which point the rickety structure imploded and 'the shadow side of wealth' was revealed. It was 'payback' time (Atwood, 2008).

Most of the paying back is being done by the public: through stimulus packages and 'quantitative easing' (whereby public reserves are drawn on so that banks can increase their cash reserves and thereby expand their lending). 'Unlike the Great Depression,' as Skidelsky (2009, 5) points out, 'governments have introduced reflationary packages, which at least promise that the slump will not spiral all the way down into a deep depression as in the 1930s'. That would appear to be in the public interest, although it is the public that is picking up a huge burden of debt the consequences of which will be experienced for decades to come. (In October 2008 the British government announced it was putting up £37 billion of public money to shore up distressed banks – and that was only the start.) However, the 'blame games' as Skidelsky (2009, 22–28) calls them – blaming the bankers, the credit-rating agencies, the hedge funds, the central bankers, the regulators, the governments – only get us so far. The 'real failure', he argues, lies elsewhere: 'to understand the crisis we need to get beyond the blame game. For at the root of the crisis was not failures of character or competence, but a failure of ideas'.

Inequality, Inequality, Inequality

Freedom is not the theoretical right to enjoy privileges of which, in practice, we are unable to take advantage. To pretend that, because there is no legal prohibition on

such activities, the children of the inner cities are free to go to Eton and that their
grandparents are free to enjoy Caribbean cruises is a cruel deception. Freedom is
the practical ability to make the choices which we wish to make.

(Hattersley, 2004, 12)

Over half a century ago Trilling (1951, 303) insisted in *The Liberal Imagination* that we must learn 'to think of ideas as living things, inescapably connected with our wills and desires, as susceptible of growth and development by their very nature, as showing their life by their tendency to change, as being liable, by this very tendency, to deteriorate and become corrupt and to work harm'. Ideas do sometimes fail and when they fail the moral and political consequences may be extremely damaging. The failure of ideas alluded to above was one such failure: a moral failure based on a misplaced assumption – namely, that markets exist for every possible contingency and that they should therefore be unregulated and free of all state intervention. Underlying that misplaced assumption was a Disney-esque fantasy that Hattersley (as quoted above) exposes: freedom is achieved not, as the fantasists maintained, through some abstract right of unlimited choice, but through 'the practical ability to make the choices which we wish to make'. If the options are not available, then the choices cannot be made – and no amount of rhetoric regarding freedom of choice can change that undeniable fact. Our freedoms are solidly framed by a reality that is not entirely of our own making.

Although associated in the UK with the Thatcher years, New Labour bought heavily into the deregulation formula and the myth of unconstrained free choice. By their influence on the way policymakers think about the world, the proponents of these ideas that have so spectacularly failed helped create a system which Skidelsky (2009, 32) characterizes as 'inefficient, unjust and prone to frequent collapses'. Its inefficiency and proneness to collapse were neatly summarized by the then governor of the Bank of England who at the height of the crisis declared that: 'not since the beginning of the First World War has our banking system been so close to collapse' (King, 2008, 2). However, the injustice of the system is equally disturbing, not only in its creation of gross inequalities between sections of society, but also in its reliance on the rise of inequality as a necessary feature of economic growth. Perversely, deregulation factored into its formula of economic success an exponential rise in inequality across society. What was viewed as an increasingly classless society became an increasingly unequal – and increasingly unjust – society.

It may no longer be possible to calibrate inequality in terms of traditional class differentials. The differentials nevertheless exist, with those at the extreme ends of the social spectrum experiencing either the depths of barely sustainable poverty or the heights of incalculable wealth. (The poorest have no difficulty knowing what they are worth, since they possess nothing or less than nothing; the wealthiest have difficulty in calculating their wealth, since their assets accrue second by second.) 'At the top', suggests Wright (2009, 114), '[is] an extremely rich capitalist class and corporate managerial class, living at extraordinarily high consumption standards, with relatively weak constraints on their exercise of economic power'; at the bottom is 'a pattern of interaction between race and class in which the working poor and the marginalized population are disproportionately made up of racial minorities'. How we characterize these extremes is open to question and to theoretical speculation. That the gap between the extremes is widening and has been for the past thirty years is an incontrovertible fact.

As Toynbee and Walker (2009, 6–7) point out, within the UK the gap between rich and poor is particularly marked:

> the UK was and remains far less equitable than other European Union countries. While the top 10% of income earners get 27.3% of the cake, the bottom 19% get just 2.6%. Twenty years ago the average chief executive of one of the top hundred companies on the FTSE index earned 17 times the average employee's pay. By 2008, the typical FTSE boss earned 75.5 times the average.

Moreover, Toynbee and Walker estimate that as a group the wealthiest pay less in tax than the tax payers in the lowest income bracket: 'take the 1,000 people who appeared in the *Sunday Times* Rich List for 2007 . . . If in 2007 Her Majesty's Revenue and Customs had secured the 10% of their capital gains and 40% of their higher-bracket income as Parliament ordained, the Treasury would have been better off by £12 billion, simply by collecting what is avoided' (2009, 18).

However, not even the UK can compete with the USA in the accumulation of inequality. As Judt (2009/2010, 88) points out, 'in the US today, the "Gini coefficient" – a measure of the distance separating rich and poor – is comparable to that of China'. The comparison is significant, argues Judt, because it runs counter to the grand narratives of opportunity and aspiration that characterize 'the American dream': 'when we consider that China is a developing country where huge gaps will inevitably open up between the wealthy few and the impoverished many, the fact that here in the US we have a similar inequality coefficient says much about how far we have fallen behind our earlier aspirations' (p. 88). (See Khan, 2009, for a study of the wider international impact of inequality and poverty.) Insofar as those earlier aspirations pointed towards a more just and equal society – a reduction in the gap between 'the wealthy few and the impoverished many' – then the last three decades undoubtedly mark a collective failure. We have become accustomed to injustice and inequality. 'We have', comments Judt, 'adapted all too well and in consensual silence' (p. 88).

Encroaching Privatization

I never cease to be surprised at the sheer lunacy of the neocon project . . . It should have been apparent from quite early on that neoliberal fundamentalism produced an enormous instability in the operations of capitalism.

(Hobsbawm, 2010, 133–135)

Why? How can we explain this adaptation? What can account for this 'consensual silence'? Judt argues that a large part of the reason is to be found in the process of privatization: 'in the last thirty years, a cult of privatisation has mesmerized Western (and many non-Western) governments' (p. 88). Like any cult, the 'cult of privatisation' presents itself as an enlightenment project: an exit route from the dark cave of unknowing. In this case the dark cave is budgetary constraint and privatization the exit route. Privatization appears to save money: 'if the state owns an inefficient public program or an expensive public service – a waterworks, a car factory, a railway – it seeks to offload it onto private buyers' (p. 88). Not only will the private buyers reduce public expenditure, but they will also manage the expensive public service – the energy utility, the public transport system – with so much more efficiency than their public sector counterparts. These, anyway, are the articles of faith to which the 'cult of privatisation' would have us assent – and as a consequence of which, in Monbiot's (2001) apt phrase, we have acquiesced to 'the corporate takeover of Britain'.

There are four good reasons for challenging these articles of faith, three of which are spelt out by Judt. First, privatization is in practice inefficient. Governments almost invariably pass into the private sector only those public goods that are running at a loss. Consequently the state sells cheap and the public takes the loss. During the Thatcher-era alone, claims Judt,

£14 billion were lost to the UK taxpaying public through the sale of public assets to the private sector (p. 88). Second, there arises the question of what Judt calls 'moral hazard'. Since the state routinely minimizes or eliminates the private investors' exposure to risk by protecting them against serious loss ('thereby undermining the classic case for privatization: that the profit motive encourages efficiency'), the private sector is likely to prove at least as inefficient as its public counterpart. The investors are onto a non-loser: 'creaming off such profits as are to be made and charging losses to the state' (p. 88). Third, privatized provisions remain the responsibility of the public authorities. The economic profit accrues to the private investors, but the losses are borne by the state which is also ultimately responsible for the quality of the privatized services: 'even after they are sold, they cannot be left to the vagaries of the market. They are inherently the sort of activity that *someone* has to regulate' (original emphasis) (p. 92).

The fourth and possibly most telling case against privatization is that it deprives the public of its own collective responsibility for the provision of essential services. Collective responsibility cannot by definition be privatized. At best the process of privatization reduces collective responsibility to a system of state regulation (which may or may not involve some measure of public consultation). That system may then in turn be out-sourced, thereby further distancing the public from the provision of services that are essential to its well being. Postal services, railway networks, retirement homes, prisons and, increasingly, schools, colleges and higher education now fall into this category of semi-private, semi-public provision. The Cabinet Office lists 790 'non-departmental public bodies' (NDPBs) – otherwise known as 'quasi-autonomous non-governmental organisations' (QUANGOs) – that comprise this twilight zone. (The Taxpayer's Alliance claims the figure is actually 1,162.) Although designated non-governmental, many of these organizations practice the policies of government and most of them are directly funded from taxes. However, they are neither government departments nor under direct ministerial control – hence the phrase 'arms length bodies' to describe their relation, or lack of it, to central government.

Hobsbawm (2010, 133), as quoted above, reminds us that these more or less local difficulties are symptoms of what he calls 'world distempers' the causes of which only became fully recognizable with 'the worldwide crisis of capitalism, which we had been predicting, but which nevertheless took a long time to occur' . That crisis cut deep into the global economy. 'Free market ideology', Stiglitz (2010, 221) insists, 'turned out to be an excuse for new forms of exploitation. "Privatization" meant that foreigners could buy mines and oil fields in developing countries at low prices. It also meant they could reap large profits from monopolies and quasi-monopolies'. The crisis also cut deep into the institutional heartlands of democratic participation and civic engagement. One of the civic spaces severely affected was higher education. The effect was heightened by the routine complicity of higher education – and, in particular, of the senior administrative and academic cadre of higher education – in the new *zeitgeist* of managerialism. As Inglis (2004, 35) puts it: 'this poison is home-made'.

The Business of Higher Education

Are universities really businesses? Are they to become forcing houses for the immediate economic development of the country and nothing else . . .? If that is what the country wants, so be it. But we should be clear that it means the end of the universities as they have been known in the West since the Middle Ages.

(*Josipovici*, 2010, 6)

One might have imagined – hoped even – that higher education would retain a critical distance from this process of creeping privatization. That was not, and is not, the case. The quotation above is taken from a letter by an eminent international scholar written to the *The Times Literary Supplement* informing its readers of an e-mail sent by the Vice-Chancellor of the University of Sussex, Michael Farthing, to all undergraduates within his institution. The email, according to Josipovici, explains to its recipients the Vice-Chancellor's plans for the development of the University – plans which include the sacking of over one hundred staff and the closing down of a number of academic areas. 'Clearly', concludes Josipovici, 'this university at any rate is being treated strictly as a business, with the least profitable branches closed and the most profitable one's developed.' At the very least, things seem to be happening in higher education without any public debate on the large philosophical and moral issues that are clearly at stake.

Higher education is increasingly located – and implicated – in the swampland of semi-private, semi-public provision: or, in officialese, the 'enabling state'. The increasing reliance on mechanisms of accountability and audit in the management of higher education is what is now most easily associated with that weasel worded phrase. However, within higher education, this reliance on the managerial mechanisms of the 'enabling state' has been complemented by the increasing reliance of higher education on *commercialization, commodification, competition* and *classification*. These four Big Cs have become its 'core business'.

Commercialization

Bok (2003, 15) analyses the process of *commercialisation* from the perspective of a seasoned senior academic, and respected legal scholar, within American higher education. Pointing to the 'rapid growth of money-making opportunities provided by a more technologically sophisticated, knowledge-based economy', Bok cites as an example the fact that, in the USA, 'corporations doubled and redoubled their share of total academic research support, increasing it from 2.3 percent in the early 1970s to almost 8 percent by the year 2000' (p. 12). 'Within a few short decades', he maintains, 'a brave new world had emerged filled with attractive possibilities for turning specialised knowledge into money' (pp. 13–14). Williams (1995, 177) points to a similar trend within the UK. 'The transformation has been dramatic', he argues: 'within ten years, students have been metamorphosed from apprentices to customers, and their teachers from master craftsmen to merchants'.

The prospect for higher education, from Bok's perspective, is bleak – and bleaker still when one recalls that a decade on his 2003 prospect is now a reality in many institutions of higher education:

> one can imagine a university of the future tenuring professors because they bring in large amounts of patent royalties and industrial funding; paying high salaries to recruit 'celebrity' scholars who can attract favourable media coverage; admitting less than fully qualified students in return for handsome parental gifts; soliciting corporate advertising to underwrite popular executive programs; promoting Internet courses of inferior quality while cancelling worthy conventional offerings because they cannot cover their costs; encouraging professors to spend more time delivering routine research services to attract corporate clients, while providing a variety of symposia and 'academic' conferences planned by marketing experts in their development offices to lure potential donors to the campus. (Bok, 2003, 200–201)

The choice, as Reid (1996) puts it, is between 'higher education or education for hire'. The complex societal forces operating in the late-modern age require a radical reappraisal of those purposes and a radical redefinition of what we understand by the increasingly differentiated and stratified public sphere: 'we need, in short, to return to the kingdom of ends' (Judt, 2009/2010, 96). However, the ways in which successive governments have set about that reappraisal and that redefinition, through the mechanisms of new public management and a collapse into wholesale commercialism, leads not to 'the kingdom of ends' but to an ideological dead-end. The chronic problem of inequality cannot be resolved through piecemeal measures that seek to reconcile centralized control with an over-reliance on unmediated market forces.

Commodification

The commercialization of higher education leads inexorably to its *commodification*. Thus, Shumar (1997) refers to the process of creeping privatization as 'the commodification of higher education', Slaughter and Leslie (1997) see it culminating in what they call 'the entrepreneurial university', while Aronowitz (2000) labels what he calls 'the corporate university' as 'the knowledge factory'. Each of these writers provides different explanations for the rapid acceleration of the process of commercialization and commodification, but they broadly agree on what is at stake: namely, that the academic practices associated with institutions of higher education have 'come to be valued in terms of their ability to be translated into cash or merchandise and not in other ways, such as aesthetic or recreational pleasure. Eventually the idea that there are other kinds of value is lost' (Shumar, 1997, 5). Those 'other kinds of value' become valueless; they become what Patel (2009) calls the 'value of nothing'. The choice then is reduced to one between 'market ideology vs. democratic values' (Engel, 2000); or, as Stein (2004) puts it, between 'buying in or selling out'.

Within the UK that problem has been exacerbated by a research assessment exercise that grades the quality of research in universities and on the basis of that grading distributes the funds available differentially across institutions. The current round of the exercise – termed the Research Excellence Framework (REF) – is not dissimilar to previous rounds, but has redefined and significantly increased the weighting given to what it calls 'impact'. For the purposes of this exercise, 'impact' does not include intellectual influence on other scholars and researchers or influence on the content of teaching. Nor does it include incidental uptake by research users outside higher education. The impact must be, and be seen to be, the outcome of a university department's own efforts to exploit or apply the research findings. It must be the direct result of a marketing ploy which seeks to commodify research and scholarship and then commercialize it as a profitable commodity.

As Collini (2009, 19) points out, this significant element within the REF involves 'some straightforward conceptual mistakes'. For example,

> the exercise conflates the notions of 'impact' and of 'benefit'. It proposes no way of judging whether an impact is desirable . . . It also confines the notion of a 'benefit' to something that is deliberately aimed at and successfully achieved . . . In terms of this exercise, research plus marketing is not just better than research without marketing: it is better *research*. (original emphasis)

He also makes the broader point that over the last three decades those in higher education have become inured to what he calls 'the proliferation of economic officialese – "user satisfaction", "market forces", "accountability", and so on'. Public discussion of the role of higher education is becoming reduced to these 'vulgarised versions' of what constitute research and scholarship. (See McKibbin, 2010, for a similar analysis.)

This officialese, argues McKibbin (2006, 6), is symptomatic of a language which is instrumental in the 'destruction of the public sphere'. It is a language which

> purports to be neutral: thus all procedures must be 'transparent' and 'robust', everyone 'accountable'. It is hard-nosed but successful because the private sector on which it is based is hard-nosed and successful. It is efficient: it abhors waste; it provides all the answers . . . The language may be laughable, but it is now the language of all those who command . . . and is one way they wield power.

It is also a language which co-opts and appropriates some of the good old words, such as 'excellence', so that 'our ears no longer hear what a fatuous, weaselly phrase "Research Excellence Framework" actually is' (Collini, 2009, 19). What Engel (2000) calls 'the struggle for the control of public education' is also a struggle for a public language of – and for – education (See Nixon, 2004; 2007). Excellence – the word and the thing itself – has become a commodity that can be bought and sold in an increasingly competitive market place.

Competition

Within the UK *competition* across the higher education sector has led to
institutional stratification and the self-protective groupings of institutions
which lobby intensively for their market niche. Institutions of higher education are ranked according to a range of measures and that ranking results
in a league table with research-led institutions invariably comprising the
premier league, research-informed and teaching led universities constituting the upper echelons of the second league, teaching led institutions with
little research capacity occupying the lower reaches of the second league,
and the rest constituting a third league of institutions that are struggling
to achieve any significant research output at all. The older universities have
almost permanent and undisputed occupancy of the premier league, the
post-1992 universities are well represented across the broad span of second
league institutions, and the bottom league is occupied almost entirely by
institutions that have gained university status more recently.

The league tables are, of course, a kind of self-fulfilling prophesy whereby
those institution located at the top recruit high profile academic staff,
attract the bulk of available research funding, and select students from a
small and highly privileged pool of often privately educated applicants..
The Sutton Trust (2008), in an analysis covering over one million university student admissions during the period 2002–2006, documented for the
first time the extent to which a few individual schools supply the majority
of students to the UK's leading research universities – and with lower academic qualifications. 'Basically put', as the Chairman of the Sutton Trust
remarks in his foreword to the report, 'a student in a state school is as likely
to go on to a leading university as a student from the independent sector
who gets two grades lower at A+ level' (p. 1). (See, also, Sutton Trust, 2004.)
The social capital – or cache – of the public school entrant outbids the
academic achievements of the state school entrant. Private interest – and
privilege – wins over the common good.

The analysis, based on admissions figures for 3,700 schools with sixth
forms, sixth form colleges, and further education colleges across the
UK during the five year period, provides disturbing evidence of extreme
inequalities across the system. Focusing on a group of 13 leading research-
led institutions whose degree courses generally have the most stringent
entry requirements, the report confirmed that the feeder schools supply-
ing entrants to these universities are reserved almost exclusively for those
children from privileged backgrounds: 'independent schools – representing just 7% of schools and 15% of A-level entrants – dominate the university rankings. These schools are available to those children whose parents

can afford fees. The remaining places are taken up by state schools that are themselves socially selective – either as a consequence of academic selection or by being situated in a middle class area' (p. 18).

Moreover, of these elite feeder schools, those with the highest admission rates to the 13 leading universities are highly socially selective. The top 100 schools are, for example, composed of 83 independent (fee-paying) schools, 16 (state funded, selective) grammar schools and one (state funded) comprehensive school, while the top thirty are composed of 13 independent (fee paying) schools, 16 (state funded, selective) grammar schools and one (state funded) comprehensive school (p. 3). Figures relating to student admissions to Cambridge and Oxford Universities present a similarly bleak picture of social selection and systemic inequality. Here the top 100 schools with the highest admission rates are composed of 78 independent (fee paying) schools, 21 grammar (state funded, selective) schools, and one (state funded) comprehensive school, while the top 30 schools are composed of 29 independent (fee paying) schools and one (state funded, selective) grammar school – and not a single state funded comprehensive school in sight.

Classification

The somewhat complex classificatory sets and sub-sets distinguished in the previous paragraph are revealing of the extent to which the business of higher education is centrally concerned with the reproduction of *classification*. The inequalities evident in patterns of entry to institutions of higher education as documented above are reflected in the entry patterns to the older professions. The funnel effect whereby the privately educated gain a disproportional share of places at the leading universities has the further effect of ensuring that they fill not only a disproportionate number of posts within the older professions but also a disproportionate number of top posts within those same professions. The classificatory system is not only maintained and reproduced but becomes ever more discriminating and selective.

Thus, for example, the legal profession is top heavy with those who have been independently educated: 'our findings show that in both samples [1989 and 2004] over two thirds of barristers at the top commercial chambers went to fee-paying schools and over 80 per cent were educated at Oxford or Cambridge, while very few went to universities outside the top 12 – just seven per cent in 2004' (Sutton Trust, 2005b, 5). A similar pattern emerges from a Sutton Trust (2006) study of the educational backgrounds of leading journalists: 'over half (54%) of the country's leading news journalists were educated in private schools, which accounts for 7% of the school population as a whole' (p. 4). To argue that such individuals are appointed on merit is to miss the point: merit in such cases is, in part at least, a consequence of gross inequality.

The elected chamber of the UK houses of parliament fares better, with the Sutton Trust (2005a, 2)reporting that 'almost one third (32%) of current MPs attended independent schools, which educate just 7% of the population'. However, the Madano Partnership (2009) predicts from its ongoing survey that there will be a marked increase in the proportion of new MPs who were privately educated compared with the last intake in 1997. From their figures they forecast that a third of all new MPs will have been to fee-paying schools, compared with 13% of new arrivals when the House of Commons last underwent major change in 1997. This, as Harris (2009) remarks, is a 'striking statistic'.

At the time of writing the UK National Equality Panel has only just published its government commissioned report (Hills and others, 2010). It is not possible therefore to do its detailed and comprehensive analysis full justice. However, one of the key findings of this independent report is that inequality has a cumulative effect across the life cycle: 'we see this before children enter school, through the school years, through entry into the labour market, and on to retirement, wealth and resources for retirement, and mortality rates for later life. Economic advantage and disadvantage reinforce themselves across the life cycle, and often on to the next generation' (p. 386). This cross-generational reproduction of inequality is evident in the pattern of student achievement within higher education: 'two thirds of those with professional parents received firsts or upper seconds, but only half of those with unskilled parents. White students were the most likely to get firsts or upper seconds, and Black and Pakistani/Bangladeshi students the least likely' (p. 366).

The Public Good

Let us steer ourselves consequently by one familiar demand of the economy, and revive the ideal of an education couched in terms of our common good and our humanity!

(Beck, 2004, 56)

Widening access to higher education is undoubtedly one of the success stories of the latter half of the last century and the first decade of the twenty-first century – and might therefore be seen as a positive response to Beck's clarion call for 'an education couched in terms of our common good and our humanity'. Nevertheless, the deep codes of chronic structural inequality remain: institutional stratification across the higher education sector, the reproduction of privilege through the selective mechanisms of higher education, and the consolidation of private and professional elites. Those involved in higher education knew what was happening: academic leaders transformed themselves into managerial gurus and/or political advisors, academics kept their heads down or joined the temporary craze for post-modernist theorizing on the live wires of global networking, and a newly empowered administrative cadre bureaucratized just about everything to do with 'relations' ('external relations', 'international relations', 'internal relations', etc, etc.) 'To a once unimaginable degree,' as Inglis (2004, 34–35) remarks on the state of higher education, 'money values have come to drench and saturate the climate, the culture and ethos.' 'Money values', he argues, 'are everywhere in intellectual life.'

In the attempted 'rolling back' of the state, the idea of the authority and legitimacy of the democratic state became ever fuzzier. The authority and legitimacy of any democracy are based upon the will and participation of the people. They cannot be transferred to the vagaries of the market without putting at risk democracy itself. The democratic state exists not – as in the case of the totalitarian state – to impose its own independent will, but to interpret and mediate the will of the citizens that constitute and shape its future direction. They are its constitutions. That is why Judt (2009/2010, 92) insists that, at this particular ethical and political juncture, we not only have to stop and think, but more specifically stop and think about the constitution of the state. We must, as he puts it, 'learn to "think the state" once again' – think, that is, the 'collective interests, collective purposes, and collective goods' that constitute the state and without which the state ceases to exist as a viable democratic entity.

But how are we to think – or re-think – the state when the state has disappeared into the thick fog of semi-private, semi-public provision. How are we to locate it? How are we to relate to it? Ministers of state may inform us that the state no longer governs from a single locus of power, but devolves power through networks of governance; yet state control of higher education through admissions and funding policies and through the mechanisms of bureaucratic accountability becomes increasingly invasive. The state seems to veer unpredictably between what central government sees as a strategy of decentralized enablement and what at the institutional level is experienced as a relentlessly disabling policy of centralized control. Torn between rolling itself back and pushing itself forward, the state is increasingly out of joint. It seems unsure as to where the locus of democratic power lies.

Learning to 'think the state' means learning to think the necessary relation between the state and the public. In any democracy what is good for the state has to be for the good of the people – and what is good for the people is for the people to determine together. That is why, within a democracy, agency and citizenship are of paramount importance. Human beings form the bedrock of democracy. Their constitution as social and civic participants within the public realm is what constitutes the democratic state. That is why education matters and why higher education seen as the gateway to independent learning is of vital importance – or, to turn that argument on its head, education matters insofar as it contributes to the public good without which the democratic state becomes a hollowed-out husk.

The possibility of collective change for the future starts with a collective consciousness of the present. That necessarily involves confronting the relentless escalation of inequality within contemporary society. If at that point we stop and think, then we are faced with some stark choices that involve not only our own opportunities and freedoms but the freedoms and opportunities of others. We need the imagination to rethink the state in terms of revitalized modes of social, civic and cosmopolitan engagement; but we also need the conditions and the resources necessary for that imaginative endeavour. The 'we' evoked here is, of course, itself part of an imagined community of those working at the transformative edge of higher education and committed to creating the institutional conditions necessary for higher education to fulfil a transformative role within a civic and increasingly cosmopolitan society. Higher education is central to imagining and resourcing an educated public with the capability, reason and purpose necessary for a sustainable future.

We return explicitly to the theme of the public good in the final chapter. The public good is not an abstraction, but the actuality of people working together for their own and others' good. That good is a 'common good', but a common good which recognizes difference; it is what we understand by the 'good society', but a good society which struggles with what goodness means in a world of difference. There is a great deal of ground to cover before we arrive, in the final chapter, at the theme of the return of the public. However, the progression of the argument across the following chapters is towards a notion of the public good as grounded in what we are as human beings. Higher education has its roots in the grounds of actuality.

***

The following three chapters (Chapters 2–4) set about the task of imagining 'the public' in terms of three of its present and future trajectories: the *social*, *civic* and *cosmopolitan* imaginaries. Human beings are social, civic and cosmopolitan by nature. It is this ontological grounding that makes the public realm a necessary reality. In becoming ourselves we necessarily reach out to others. Higher education facilitates, encourages and sustains this process of becoming worldly: learning to care for the world in all its difference. What I term 'the public' has to be imagined for each new generation, since its old formulations sediment and its old structures harden. Higher education is one of the spaces within which we are able to set about this imaginative task of learning to live together in a world of difference and thereby reclaim the public realm as a shared space of human action. That task of imaginative reclamation and reconstruction is one of the most important and urgent tasks facing higher education in the twenty-first century.

Chapter 2

Social Imaginaries

Our social imaginary at any time is complex. It incorporates a sense of the normal expectations that we have of each other; the kind of common understanding which enables us to carry out the collective practices which make up our social life. This incorporates some sense of how we all fit together in carrying out the common practice.

(*Taylor, 2007, 172*)

Public education is a necessity, not an optional extra. It contributes, crucially, to the wellbeing of society as a whole and is therefore a matter of public concern. As such, it should be seen as a common, public good, not a privately owned commodity – which is why those key phrases of Taylor ('common understanding', 'collective practices', 'social life', 'common practice') are of such vital importance. Aristotle (1992, 452), in concluding his exposition on politics, was adamant on this point: 'education must be one and the same for all, and . . . the responsibility for it must be a public one, not the private affair it now is . . . In matters that belong to the public, training for them must be the public's concern.' Aristotle's argument at this point in *The Politics* is premised on his view that human beings are, by nature, political creatures: 'it is not right either that any of the citizens should think that he belongs just to himself; he must regard all citizens as belonging to the state, for each is a *part* of the state; and the responsibility for each part naturally has regard to the responsibility for the whole' (p. 452). If, by nature, humans exist in civic association as part of a polity, then the question of how to live together is central to individual survival. That question, argues Aristotle, is the prime concern of public education: education conceived, that is, as the means by which we learn to grow into our common humanity.

Curran (2000) reminds us that Aristotle's insistence on the necessity of public education remains both relevant and highly contested. Education is increasingly located within, and funded through, the mechanisms of the marketplace; and, more insidiously, through the sponsorship of special interest groups, particularly faith groups. It is seen as a private commodity, at best a family investment; not as a communal good, a shared interest in a common future. The radical alternatives, envisaged by Aristotle, still require immense leaps of the imagination: *social imaginaries, civic imaginaries* and *cosmopolitan imaginaries*. This and the following two chapters begin to trace those public imaginaries. In doing so, they point to a new ethics of education: an ethics of magnanimity, of reaching out, of generosity. We start, where we shall finish, with the old (but still dazzlingly new) idea of human being and human becoming as essentially communal, associative and affiliative: 'for each part naturally has regard to the responsibility for the whole'. Persons attain personhood by virtue of being persons-in-relation. There is, as Aristotle insisted, no other way of growing-up.

This and the following two chapters set about the task of 'imagining' the relation between higher education and the public good. The latter, I argue, is not simply a fortuitous consequence of the educational process, but informs and shapes both its origins and purposes. To flourish educationally is to grow – as a person, a citizen, and a member of an emergent *cosmopolis* – into the public good. This opening chapter focuses on the idea of being human as being socially constituted and on the implications of this idea for how we should conceive of the role of education in human formation and human flourishing. It argues that, since the self is *naturally* social and sustained through mutuality and reciprocity, the well being of the individual is necessarily a public good the underlying ethic of which is one of mutual recognition. Human being – what we are – is always in a process of becoming, because as human beings we are *by nature* social beings located in time: persons-in-relation. The defence of education as a public good starts on the firm if somewhat slippery ground of ontology: with what we are and where we might begin; how we define and distinguish ourselves as human beings; and, crucially, why the recognition of what Ricoeur (1994) terms 'oneself as another' is fundamental to the task of human formation and flourishing.

La Vie Commune

Sociability is neither accidental nor contingent; it is the very definition of the human condition.

(*Todorov, 2002, 86*)

We shall turn to Ricoeur's arguments on this subject in due course. We rely initially, however, on some of the distinctions drawn by an anthropologist with a deep and abiding commitment to pursuing ontological questions regarding what it means to be human. Todorov (1995) sees humanity as layered: rather like an onion. The outer layer it shares with everything that comprises the material world. This outer layer he terms 'being'. Beyond that layer is what he terms 'life', which is what we share with all other living forms: lichen, amoeba, hummingbirds, etc. Humanity, however, has a further ontological layer, which Todorov terms 'existence'. To exist as a human being is to be socially constituted. Human beings do not discover their individuality and then become social; they achieve identity in and through the social: the unity of the human life – its unique narrative form – is, as Todorov puts it, *la vie commune*. To be human is to be part of the material world, part of the living and reproducing world, but, also, part of the complex social nexus that comprises whatever it is that is unique to human existence.

The terminology may lose some of its nuance in translation, but Todorov's notion of layering is nevertheless highly suggestive. So conceived, humanity is, to switch metaphor, a palimpsest. Only the final layer of the palimpsest, however, ascribes to the human animal its humanity. This is the layer of being together, of being defined through community and communication, and expressed through the uniquely human resources of language and speech. One of the indisputable legacies of the European Enlightenment, argues Todorov (2002, 82), is the humanistic insight into the human self as constitutively social: 'what matters is that human beings do not live and cannot live outside of society. To believe that they are asocial by nature is an aberration; to imagine that their goal is to become asocial is to indulge in illusions'. The defining ends and purposes of being human are social, communal and associative.

So, too, insists Todorov, are its origins: human beings begin in the social, in the middle and muddle of things: 'the specifically human action is the gaze of mutual recognition . . . It follows that "others" are immediately present within the human. This statement could also be reformulated by saying that without consciousness, man is not man; and consciousness is the effect of communication, of our internalization of being taken into consideration by others' (pp. 87–88). Communication is not effected by consciousness; consciousness is the effect of our growing capacity to communicate. My consciousness, as a human being, is contingent upon my communicative capabilities as a human being born into a world of other human beings who are similarly possessed of communicative competence.

From earliest infancy my attachment to others forms the very substance of my life. This is how we are: 'born incomplete, dying incomplete, always prey to the need for others, always in quest of the missing complement'; we are 'constitutionally and definitively incomplete'. It is because we come into existence 'congenitally incomplete' that we need others, need to be considered, need attachment (p. 89).

In spite of his insistence on the individual as incomplete, deficit, not-yet-finished, Todorov nevertheless argues that 'relations with others augment the self instead of diminishing it'. This human characteristic of incompletion is what makes us what we are. It is the source of our virtues and our vices, of our discontents, and of our 'fragile happiness' (p. 90). Our lack of completion as isolated entities is what allows us to grow into the plenitude of persons-in-relation: 'in the network of human relations, no isolated entities exist but only relations; the very opposition between essence and accident has no place in the world of intersubjectivity. In personal life, the person in himself does not exist' (p. 93). Selfhood is 'necessarily shifting' because there is, necessarily, 'a permeability between self and other' (p. 141). The legacy of humanism, argues Todorov, is the idea that we can only flourish and achieve well being in what he terms the 'imperfect garden' of social relations.

Todorov fixes on this point because, as he argues, *modernity* is so often equated exclusively with *individualism*, which is in turn equated with individual *choice*, which is then taken to be the defining feature of *liberalism*, which in its turn is taken to be the *sine qua non* of Western *democracy* (in the interests of which non-compliant states are systematically bombed back into pre-modernity). It is true, as Todorov acknowledges, that 'the inhabitant of contemporary society . . . wants to know the world on her own, and demands that whole swathes of existence should be governed by the principles she chooses.' As he rightly points out, 'the elements of her life are no longer all *givens* in advance; some of them are *chosen*' (p. 9). It is also true, however, that self-interested choice is irrational; rational choice, if not necessarily collective, must take account of the fact that countless others are making choices and acting upon those choices with unknown and unknowable consequences. My agency must recognize your agency, and your agency must recognize my agency, if we are both to lead sustainable and flourishing lives.

If, as Todorov argues, human life is by definition communal – *la vie commune* – then the well being of the person is a matter of public concern: the good of the part is necessarily the good of the whole. It follows that insofar as education contributes to the well being and flourishing of the person, it necessarily contributes to the public good. To argue otherwise would be to reject the idea that 'sociability is . . . the very definition of the human condition' (p. 86) or to deny that education has any significance in the development of personhood. The argument advanced in this book assumes in other words, not only (as Todorov maintains) that human beings are by nature social, but also that the social well being of human beings is one of the prime ends and purposes of education. It is to that second strand of the argument that we shall now turn by way, initially, of the notion of mutual recognition as elaborated by Honneth (1995) and Ricoeur (2005).

Recognition and Mutuality

The fact that the possibility of a positive relation-to-self emerges only with the experience of recognition can be interpreted as pointing to necessary conditions for individual self-realization.

(Honneth, 1995, 173–174)

Ricoeur (2005), building on Honneth's insights into 'the experience of recognition', sees recognition as a 'course', a process, the trajectory of which can be described in terms of its linguistic usage within philosophical discourse: 'my hypothesis is that potential philosophical uses of the verb *to recognize* can be organised along a trajectory running through its use in the active voice to its use in the passive voice' (p. 19). This 'reversal on the grammatical plane' he goes on to argue, shows 'the traces of a reversal of the same scope on the philosophical plane' (p. 19). Thus, to recognize in the active voice – 'to recognise as an act' – 'expresses a pretension, a claim, to exercise an intellectual mastery over this field of meanings, of signifying assertions'; while, at the opposite end of the trajectory, recognition in the passive voice – the demand to be recognized – 'expresses an expectation that can be satisfied only by mutual recognition, where this mutual recognition either remains an unfulfilled dream or requires procedures and institutions that elevate recognition to the political plane' (p. 19). The moral compass points towards mutuality, reciprocity, inter-dependence.

This 'course of recognition', as outlined by Ricoeur, goes something like this: from a process of 'recognition as identification' – recognizing other things in the world; through a process of 'recognising oneself' – identifying oneself in the world; to a process of 'mutual recognition' – being recognized as the object of other's identification. Ricoeur's grammatical analogy – from active to passive voice – is not intended to imply a movement from agency to lack of agency, but is attempting to locate the agent within a broader spectrum – or grammar – of mutuality and reciprocity: I become a person through an overlapping process which involves me in differentiating things in a world out there, identifying myself as an element within that differentiated world, and acknowledging that myriad others are involved in this process of mutual recognition. It is in part a life saga of the passage from cradle to birth; but also something of a psycho drama involving the historical layering of that saga in the here and now. To follow the grammatical analogy, the relation between the 'I' and the 'me' – the 'I' as identifying agent and the 'me' as identified subject – is mutually dependent: 'I' has no validity without a 'me', and 'me' has no substance without an 'I'. We each flourish – grow and distinguish ourselves – one with another.

Ricoeur's 'course' is, then, a kind of lifelong curriculum, a curriculum-in-the-making: a *curriculum vitae*. An underlying principle of this curriculum-not-yet-finished is that becoming and knowing cannot be unravelled into the tidy compartments of ontology and epistemology. Being, becoming and knowing are complicatedly entangled, knotted: what I am – and become – is what and how I know; what and how I know is what I am – and become. Ricoeur is suggesting that when and if ever we come to untangle the knot, the notion of mutual recognition may be a useful starting point – and, also, an end point: 'the course of self-recognition ends in mutual recognition' (Ricoeur, 2005, 107). The recognition of self involves recognition of others who in turn confer selfhood upon oneself as another: that, in part at least, is what Ricoeur means by human development through the mutuality and reciprocity of recognition. We grow up through an understanding of ourselves as differentiated, sentient beings within a world of other differentiated, sentient beings.

Honneth (1995, 129) schematizes this course of recognition in terms of particular 'forms of recognition': 'primary relationships' of love and friendship (involving 'needs and emotions'); 'legal relations' of human rights (involving 'moral responsibility'); and relations of solidarity achieved through 'communities of value' (involving individual 'traits and abilities'). One of the implications of this schema is that social cohesion is dependent upon relationships that acknowledge needs and emotions. Social cohesion undoubtedly involves legal frameworks and cultural solidarities, but is premised upon the primacy of inter-dependency. Dependency is, paradoxically, *the* defining characteristic of the human agent: agency is always enacted within a force field of conflicting needs and interests.

We are needy by nature, hence what Honneth terms 'the struggle for recognition': 'persons can feel themselves to be "valuable" only when they know themselves to be recognized for accomplishments that they precisely do not share in an undifferentiated manner with others' (p. 125). My value to myself lies in your recognition of my difference; your value to yourself lies in my recognition of your difference. To be human is to crave difference *and* to desire the commonality necessary for our differences to be mutually recognized. Not to have one's difference recognized is a form of disrespect, which (argues Honneth) expresses itself in acts of abuse and rape, exclusion and the denial of human rights, and denigration and insult; the recognition of difference, on the other hand, is a precondition of 'basic self-confidence', 'self-respect' and 'self-esteem' (p. 129). To flourish is to have the capabilities and to enjoy the institutional conditions necessary for engaging in this 'struggle for recognition'.

What Honneth (1991; 1995) and Ricoeur (1994; 2005) understand by 'the course of recognition' or 'the struggle for recognition' is the process of realizing one's own humanity – the process of human flourishing. It points us in the direction of what Honneth (1995, 173–174) refers to as the 'necessary conditions for individual self-realization'. The part that formal education plays in establishing and sustaining these necessary conditions is the subject of this book and particularly the central chapters (Chapters 5–7 inclusive). At this early point in the argument we need to acknowledge that how we define the ends and purposes of education must be in the light of our understanding of this common process of self-realization through mutual recognition – and to begin to establish what those ends and purposes might be.

Social Well Being

The oak cannot return to the condition of the acorn.

(Berlin, 1996, 4)

Human life is narrative in form: each of us is a unique trajectory. We are creatures in and of time. What we share, and what defines our commonality, is the experience of becoming uniquely ourselves, uniquely individualized: that is the paradox that informs and structures the human narrative.

A number of consequences follow from this primary insight. First, the precise course of the individual trajectory cannot be predetermined because it both acts upon and is responsive to the trajectories of others. The outcomes of individual actions cannot be pre-specified with complete certainty. To live a life entirely devoid of human unpredictability would be to have no life at all. We may seek to minimize the risk of the unpredictable through the exercise of wise choice, deliberation and circumspection, but the unpredictable – and therefore the un-pre-specifiable – is nevertheless always with us.

Second, we cannot unlearn what life has taught us; cannot entirely undo what we have done and what others have done; we cannot perform a backward somersault into what we once were. As Berlin (1996) in his essay entitled 'a sense of reality' famously remarked, 'the oak cannot return to the condition of the acorn'. The cost of our flourishing as human agents is the irreversibility of the consequences that necessarily flow from our actions. Third, our unique narratives necessarily intertwine: they are both deeply personal and profoundly communal. We flourish together or not at all, acquiring and requiring an interdependent ecology of well being – what Barnett (1999) terms a condition of super-complexity in which not only our theories and institutions and larger systems are contestable, but also our meta-theories and our frameworks of understanding the world. Growing up is largely a matter of learning how to grow together in a world of increasing complexity: how to support our own agency and that of others, how to build communities of understanding and value, how to co-exist.

To locate education within this process is to recognize, with Williams (1989, 14), that education is ordinary: 'that it is, before everything else, the process of giving to the ordinary members of society its full common meanings, and the skills that will enable them to amend these meanings, in the light of their personal and common experience'. Education is what we human beings do when we are becoming human; when we are becoming citizens; when we are learning to care for the world. Social well being is both a condition, and a constitutive element, of education: education contributes to my social well being which in turn provides the conditions necessary for my continuing educational development.

To educate is necessarily to educate for social well being. A system of higher education that did not contribute to social well being would be inconceivable – a contradiction in terms. Whatever is educational about higher education is centrally concerned with social well being. It is centrally concerned, that is, with the necessary relation between: (1) education and becoming – human flourishing; (2) education and individualization – human personhood; and (3) education and relationship – human inter-dependency. These three necessary components of social well being lie at the heart of higher education.

Education and becoming: human flourishing

Since the death of Socrates in 399 BC, the architects and visionaries of civil society have had to acknowledge that what we know – and, crucially, what we do not know – is what we are: I am what I think (and what I know to be unthinkable). The Socratic presence that is transmitted through the Platonic dialogues (which is almost the only recorded presence we have) is, like us, an endless chatterbox. The 'talkativeness' of Socrates, as Wilson (2007, 193) puts it, 'identified him as a modern person: like us he talked too much'. Insofar as this talkativeness is – and was – part of the enduring Socratic legacy, it is centrally concerned with the necessary complementarities of two very different precepts: how what we think we know accords with, or is discordant with, how we act.

That was Socrates' core question: how do I know that what I am doing well is the right thing to be doing? As an Athenian veteran of the prolonged and bloody Peloponnesian War – which, accompanied by plague and famine, shook the fledgling Athenian democracy to its foundations – Socrates knew all too well that knowing what is the right thing to do and doing the right thing well are both different and complementary. Waging the right wars and conducting them well are, as generals on occasion have the unenviable task of pointing out to prime ministers and presidents, very different kinds of thing. The ethical imperative is both to do the right thing and to do the right thing well. Socrates was required to drink Hemlock – a gentlemanly mode of execution by the standards of the day – because he refused to compromise on precisely that imperative.

Higher education must develop individuals who are not only efficient and effective in the use of their acquired knowledge, but who can use that knowledge to make complex choices regarding the right uses and applications of that knowledge. This has pedagogical implications in that education becomes a process whereby knowledge and understanding are mediated – not simply transmitted. Knowing cannot be reduced to the passive reception of supposed facts, since it necessarily involves a complex process of accommodation and critical engagement: what I know, and what I do not know, determine my horizons, shape my possible futures, and define my agency. My knowledge and understanding of the world are indispensable constituents of my social well being: I define my actions through self understanding and the understanding of self in relation to others. In so doing, I grow and develop. I flourish.

Education and individuation: human personhood

Similarly, my knowledge and understanding of the world – how I uniquely assimilate and accommodate myself to that knowledge – differentiate and distinguish me. In a highly differentiated society such as ours, individuals shift between what Beck and Beck-Gernsheim (2002, 23) term 'functional spheres'. Some of these spheres 'are neither interchangeable nor graftable onto one another'. Consequently, 'people are integrated into society only in their partial aspects as taxpayers, car drivers, students, consumers, voters, patients, producers, fathers, mothers, sisters pedestrians and so on'. Under these circumstances, people 'are forced to take into their hands that which is in danger of breaking into pieces: their own lives'. Gaining 'a life of one's own' – achieving personhood – requires an understanding of how one's life narrative is a story of migrations across and 'between different, partly incompatible logics of action'.

The understanding of how these peregrinations can be navigated is a necessary condition of my individuation within – and my integration into – a highly differentiated world of 'functional spheres'. As such it is central to my own and others' social wellbeing: the well being, that is, of persons-in-relation. Higher education is necessarily concerned with providing the capabilities necessary for functioning within these separate 'spheres'; it is also, however, increasingly concerned with providing the understanding necessary for functioning across these disparate 'logics of action'. This lateral and integrative understanding defines the integrity of my own and others' personhood. Without such understanding our lives would, indeed, be 'in danger of breaking into pieces'. Social well being would, at that hypothetical endpoint, become inconceivable.

Higher education must realize itself as one of the custodians of a mode of understanding which privileges the notion of 'a life of one's own'. To own one's life is to grasp its narrative unity across a highly differentiated society. We exist in a plurality of identities, and the plurality is important. As Sen (2007, 16–17) points out, 'our shared humanity gets savagely challenged when our differences are narrowed into one devised system of uniquely powerful categorization'. We are, in Sen's phrase, 'diversely different' (p. xiv) and must resist 'the miniaturization of human beings' (p. 185) that arises from the illusion of a single, homogenizing identity. Nevertheless, we need to make sense of those diverse differences that are not just a part of our external topographies, but integral to our internal landscapes. We require a sense of our own unifying personhood: an awareness of self that equates to harmony in music.

Education and relationship: human inter-dependency

Human well being is by definition social, since human beings necessarily exist in relation to one another. Personhood requires integrity and individualization, but it also requires the capacity to reach out to others. In that sense human beings are not just rational animals, but in MacIntyre's (1999) phrase 'dependent rational animals'. As such, we require the acquisition of both independence and acknowledged dependence through 'networks of giving and receiving' (p. 146). The idea that we necessarily reduce our humanity through our neediness is perfidious. Autonomy is only possible in a society in which the needs of particular groups and individuals are met. A welfare state is not a 'nanny state', but a democratic state that takes democracy seriously. The balance may be a difficult one to strike in highly competitive and deeply inequitable societies, but the interplay between giving and receiving is nevertheless an incontestable condition of democracy.

Higher education is centrally concerned with reaching out and extending horizons, developing networks of thought and communication, pushing forward into what is only partially understood. Its reach necessarily exceeds its grasp. It operates, in other words, through a deliberative process of giving and receiving, such that the reception increases the capacity to give. That is precisely the relation between teaching and learning; a relation which depends crucially upon reciprocity and mutuality. I can only teach because I am also a learner and in the process of learning I increase my capacity as a teacher. Teaching and learning are complementary aspects of a common process. Fine teachers encourage and enable learners to deliberate and explain, to argue and persuade, to communicate their current state of understanding – to acquire, that is, some of the qualities and dispositions associated with teaching. We learn together or not at all.

Human inter-dependency is a precondition of social well being, just as higher education is one of the means by which inter-dependency is processed and achieved. Social well being, in other words, is dependent upon inter-dependencies that can only be realized through mutual understanding and the recognition of difference. Higher education, at best, privileges and sustains that mode of understanding and that process of recognition.

The key element in this formulation is the notion of mutual recognition. The university is, by definition, the place – *locus, topos* – where the diaspora of human thought and identity, aspiration and purpose, method and procedure is given a home. The ethical implications of this argument begin to be spelt out in the following section of this chapter – and are developed in the final sections of the following two chapters.

Towards an Ethics of Recognition

We need to understand our own values, if we are to judge how we in particular have good reason to act.

(Dunn, 2001, 106)

If we are social by nature, and if our social well being is dependent upon our capacity for mutual recognition, then education must be seen as morally purposeful. The ethical is not some kind of decorative buttress without which the central edifice would stand secure; it is integral to the structure as a whole. Without it, that structure would collapse. The planned provision for knowledge and mutual understanding – the system of education generally and of higher education in particular – is the dynamo that drives and motivates democratic society towards its moral ends and purposes. The argument, while focusing specifically on higher education, has implications for educational practice within a wide range of institutional settings.

What does an ethics of recognition look like in the context of educational practice generally and the system of higher education in particular? What, following an ethics of recognition, might pedagogies of recognition look like? How might educational professionals work together in the interests of an ethics of pedagogy and of pedagogies of recognition? This book returns intermittently to these central questions. They are based on the premise that, as Dunn quoted above points out, we need to understand our own values if we are to judge how in specific circumstances we in particular have good reason to act. As educational professionals, working within diverse institutional contexts, the following imperatives provide a starting point.

First, the purpose of higher education is not only, or even primarily, to accrue knowledge and understanding, but to frame a debate within which fine judgements can be made as to what constitutes useful knowledge for particular groups and individuals. That is a prime component of any ethics of recognition. What my students think they want in terms of knowledge and understanding may not be exactly what they need. However, I would be a fool to completely ignore their wants, just as they would be short sighted to entirely reject my estimate of their needs. Similarly, my research sponsors and stakeholders may think they know precisely what they want from their research team by way of knowledge and understanding, but may miss an important trick if they fail to listen to their research team regarding what may be needed to address seriously the kinds of questions that concern them.

The counter argument runs something like this: if we only accrue and impart knowledge that is deemed to be useful, how can we advance our knowledge. Surely, advancement in any field of enquiry relies on our gaining knowledge the future applications of which we cannot possibly foresee: if our search for knowledge is circumscribed by the requirements of utility, then our knowledge will be limited to the closed circle of what we already judge to be useful. Our arguments and understandings will become circular, tautological, fixed; forever justifying the premises upon which they are based and from which they cannot break free.

While the counter argument is in some ways compelling, it fails in its conceptualization of the knower as a practitioner. Knowledge and agency are complementary. My understanding of the world profoundly affects the way in which I act within it. In that sense, knowledge is by definition useful, in that it relates to what I do and how I do it. (Inert knowledge is a contradiction in terms.) Knowledge is not something 'out there' to be gathered and then utilized. Its potential utility is the reason and motivation for seeking it. We may not know the precise usage. However, we do know that in order to act in certain sorts of circumstances we may well require certain kinds of knowledge and understanding.

Five hundred years ago, for example, we might have had a hunch that at some indeterminate point in the future it would be useful – essential, even – to know whether the sun revolves around the planet earth or whether the universe as we perceive it revolves on a rather different axis. While Copernicus could not have anticipated the full implications of his hard won and costly insights, he knew that the knowledge he sought was revolutionary in its potential applications. To insist on knowledge as intrinsically useful both to the knower and to other potential users now and in the future is not necessarily a form of crude instrumentalism; it is to prioritize the notion of knowledge as practice and to recognize the specific needs and precise situation of the user. It is to recognize the knower in the knowing.

A second component of any ethics of recognition as it relates to higher education is explicitness regarding the complex and often indeterminate judgements that are routinely made by academic practitioners. Reviewing papers for academic journals, assessing and examining the work of students, advising on academic appointments and promotions, reviewing proposed courses: these are all part and parcel of academic life and require discernment and discrimination. They are also activities that may profoundly affect, either adversely or positively, the prospects of those whose work is being judged. It is not enough therefore that the judgements are sound; it is also essential that the basis on which the judgements are made are open and explicit.

The argument here is that judgements which operate according to an ethics of recognition must be rationally refutable. If I am charged with the responsibility of judging your work, you have a right to know the basis upon which I am making my judgement so that you can learn from it and if necessary challenge it. The less explicit I am regarding the basis of my judgement the more I deny your agency as a rational human being. It is sometimes a difficult balancing act, given the sensitivities surrounding the reasons for forming some of the professional judgements that have to be made. Nevertheless, we need to acknowledge that this is how power works in the formation of professional judgement: either negatively, through the monopoly of power by professionals; or positively, through the distribution of power to the public.

The institutional trap that it is all too easy to fall into at this juncture is that of bureaucratic proceduralism: if we define at the outset, precisely and exhaustively, the criteria and procedures by which professional judgements are to be made, then justice will be seen to have been done. The problem with this supposed solution, which is now part of the stock in trade of the higher education sector, is that it wholly misrepresents the complexity and indeterminacy of professional judgement. A professional judgement is by definition a considered response to the unpredictable and unforeseen. The professional is defined as such precisely because he or she can cope when the rule book no longer covers the eventuality: pre-specified criteria may be a useful guide as to how to function in most circumstances, but in the exceptional circumstances that are the true test of professionalism they may be dysfunctional.

The greater the professionalism the greater is the capacity to view all cases and circumstances as in some way exceptional. People are different; their work and achievements differ; their ends and purposes are not the same. That is what it means to be human. The criteria-driven accountability culture which currently defines the higher education sector has only served to dehumanize our institutions and reduce the complexity of professional judgement to a technical tick-list. There must be a better way of building trust, being professionally accountable, recognizing the public right to know, widening participation and understanding. To throw out the precious thing of finely tuned professional discrimination and discernment with the unworthy thing of professional hegemony is not a solution to the problem.

Human beings become: we are not ready made on arrival. A third component of any ethics of recognition as it relates to higher education is to acknowledge the unpredictability of the ways in which human beings move on and develop throughout their lives. To recognize your difference is to acknowledge your potential for change. That does not preclude my being supportive of your need for continuity, but it does require me to relate to your particular trajectory. The point and purpose of higher education is to lay out the options, provide the necessary navigational resources, and highlight the implications of the various ways forward. Higher education is centrally concerned with the ways in which people develop their life projects, negotiate their life choices, and configure their life purposes. It is, first and last, concerned with human flourishing.

Higher education is not always like that. In the past it has been difficult to access for the vast majority of the population, and the ratio of students from the lowest socio-economic backgrounds gaining entry to higher education remains a scandal. Moreover, the attrition rate remains unacceptably high particularly during the first year of undergraduate study (and, again, impacts on particular socio-economic groups of students). A system that is meant to move people forward and acknowledge their achievements does precisely the opposite for a significant proportion of the student population. Higher education has been and remains for many a stumbling block rather than a gateway of opportunity.

The problem is twofold. It lies, first, in the lack of coordination across the higher education sector as a whole. Institutions of higher education compete rather than cooperate in the education of a highly differentiated student body. Movement from one institutional setting to another, as either an undergraduate or postgraduate student, is a bureaucratic nightmare; although such a move might be in the interests of the intellectual development of the student concerned. Institutions of higher education are not joined up; they are not responsive to the needs of students across the sector; they are introspective and inward looking; they are self interested. That is a damning indictment of institutions that exist to be responsive, outward looking, and orientated to the public interest.

The second aspect of the problem is that of institutional inflexibility. Entering higher education is an increasingly expensive lottery. Either I win some academic qualification or other, or I lose everything. At postgraduate level some intermediate exit points may exist: certificate, diploma (prior to Masters); MPhil (prior to Doctorate). In the main, however, the inflexibility of the system particularly at undergraduate level means that for those students who either exit their courses of study prematurely or are judged to have failed them the experience of higher education is one of blockage and possibly regression. Far from being recognized as autonomous human beings, such students are in the main abandoned without any record of achievement of their time spent within higher education. These twin aspects of the problem are systemic: historically layered and organizationally embedded.

A fourth component of an ethics of recognition is to look beyond the institutional confines of the sector and learn to work across a wider range of educational settings and with a wider range of partners. Stakeholders in higher education need to work beyond their own sectional interests, and academic practitioners in particular need to recognize that higher education is not confined to designated institutions of higher education (important though these are). Other societies do not have a civil society that can provide the infrastructures necessary for effective and sustainable cross-institutional collaboration. Where such infrastructures exist in the form of publically accountable institutions, higher education must reach out and redefine itself institutionally across a variety of educational settings. If institutions of higher education want to remain part of the hub, they must recognize the wide variety of spokes that comprise the big wheel of educational advancement.

The fear is that in the emergent culture of higher education, with its emphasis on widening access and participation and institutional diversity, institutions of higher education will lose their autonomy. No doubt the nostalgic yearning for the university as ivory tower – the icon of exclusive, and excluding, intellectual excellence – lurks behind this fear. However, there is also a rational impulse implicit in the fear. Genuine partnerships rely on the partners understanding their role and responsibilities in the partnership and (when push comes to shove) being able to hold their corner. Good partnerships are less like a soup and more like a stew: the difference, as every half decent cook knows, is not just one of liquidity, but of allowing the ingredients to retain their distinctive flavour while providing a distinctive taste.

Working as an academic practitioner with business leaders, professional musicians and writers, civil servants, social policy makers, and a wide range of professional practitioners across the private and public sectors, has convinced me that the only kind of relationships that matter educationally are those based on a sure sense of the authority of each of the partners. The authority by which one enters a relationship is an important determinant of the strength and sustainability of that relationship and of the quality of whatever outcomes may ensue. Strong and vibrant relationships are ones in which partners acknowledge the recognition of equal worth and are committed to working through the implications of that recognition for their own practice.

An ethics of recognition is based upon the idea of human beings as intrinsically social and therefore necessarily requiring mutuality. My 'I' – my agency – is dependent upon my 'me': my selfhood as you perceive it. That selfhood is both object (my 'me') and subject (my 'I'). To grow and develop individuals have to reach out to one another. They have to sustain and develop the public spheres within which they can learn from each other, from one another, and together. Sometimes they have to create those public spheres from what might at the time seem like nothing. The resources, however, are invariably – and miraculously – available to those who care to look.

If human beings are intrinsically social and if the social is a constituent element of the public, then the aspiration to have a presence and a voice within the public sphere is a defining feature of humanity. This is not to deny the human importance of privacy and intimacy, which in the modern (post-Romantic) era has gained increasing significance in the formation of selfhood and identity. We no longer equate privacy with privation as the citizens of ancient Athens would have done. However, the argument developed in this and the following two chapters insists that human beings develop their humanity by continually extending their social reach beyond the grasp of their given relations: without the intimacy and indeed privacy afforded by those given relations, the confidence to reach out and extend those relations would be seriously impaired; without the impulse to reach out and extend one's self beyond the scope of one's existing relations, those relations themselves would fail to grow and develop.

***

Education originates in these basic ontological stirrings of the self in relation to others (*la vie commune*). In advanced societies education becomes formalized into a series of institutionalized phases (for example, preschool, primary school, secondary school, post-compulsory education, higher education). Higher education is premised upon certain educational preconditions and represents a transitional phase in the process of formal education: just as early years education provides an entry into that process, so higher education provides an exit. However, education does not begin and end with these formal rites of passage. Its beginnings are grounded in the social imaginary which is in turn one arc of a broader trajectory that includes civic and cosmopolitan imaginaries. In the following chapter we follow that trajectory through the arc of the civic imaginary.

Chapter 3

Civic Imaginaries

This city will follow you.

(Cavafy, 2008)

The previous chapter argued that human beings are by nature social and that this constituent element of human being necessitates a public sphere within which we can interact, negotiate, agree and disagree, but above all flourish and become ourselves through mutual recognition. In this chapter I argue that in defining human beings as social, we are necessarily defining ourselves as citizens. We build the civic spaces which render our societies sustainable and defensible. A society requires, and therefore builds and finds the wherewithal to sustain, a polity that is by definition bound by the bonds and freedoms of civil society and the constraints and liberties of governance. Education is central to this process: it sustains, and is sustained by, a polity that in turn requires the institutional infrastructure of a civil society. It also provides the resources of civic regeneration necessary for that task.

It is to an ethics of civic engagement that we need to look for an elaboration of the necessary relation between higher education and the public good. The civic, as Cavafy intimates, follows the social: the civic imaginary flies in the slipstream of the social imaginary. Cities, townships and civic communities are, to shift metaphor, constructed on the foundations of existing cultures and societies. No system of governance is sustainable without civil society and no civil society is sustainable without some form, or forms, of human association. Human beings are not only social by nature; they are also civic by inclination; and, therefore, public by necessity. Survival amounts to the clear option between learning to live together and deciding not to live. The crucial question is how we can live together in difference. Higher education must help pose that question, address it, and inform the debates surrounding it.

The *Polity*

The public realm, as the common world, gathers us together and yet prevents us from falling over each other, so to speak.

(Arendt, 1998, 52)

If the social imaginary of education is rooted in 'la vie commune', then its civic imaginary is located in the idea of the polity: the public realm, the common ground. Arendt (1998) begins her great exposition of 'the human condition', first published in 1958, with a detailed discussion of the public and the private realms and of the distinction between them. Her politics and her ethics are firmly rooted in this distinction. The term 'public', she argues, suggests two closely interrelated meanings. It means, first, 'that everything that appears in public can be seen and heard by everybody and has the widest possible publicity' (p. 50). That phrase, 'the widest possible publicity', is significant. It suggests not just the necessary openness and transparency of the public realm, but also its expansiveness: the idea that, in the interests of its own sustainability, the public realm necessarily extends itself. It is forever seeking to push forward its own boundaries; to become increasingly inclusive; to bring more and more into the open. The public is nothing if not hegemonic.

Second, suggests Arendt, 'the term "public" signifies the world itself, in so far as it is common to all of us and distinguished from our privately owned place in it' (p. 52). What that commonality means is explained as follows: 'to live together in the world means essentially that a world of things is between those who have it in common, as a table is located between those who sit around it' (p. 52). The world is an 'in-between' that at once relates us and at the same time separates us. It is, however, a world of our own making: 'a world of things' that we hold in common. Things like tables are what we make; they are our fabrications; the products of our labour. They have their own longevity. No common world, no public realm, is conceivable, if it is erected for one generation and planned for the living only. It must have a sense of futurity, possibility, potential, unpredictability, purposefulness. By definition this little world of ours is magnanimous. It is inclusive.

Arendt concludes her discussion of the public and private realm with the thought that 'the *polis* was for the Greeks, as the res *publica* was for the Romans, first of all their guarantee against the futility of individual life, the space protected against this futility and reserved for the relative permanence, if not immortality, of mortals' (p. 56). The *polis* – or the *res publica* – is the table around which we sit together: the product of our making, the thing that is hewn and made, the artefact. It does not come ready made. The public realm is both the product of our making and the means by which, together, we produce things that are mutually beneficial. The public sphere reaches out: spatially and temporally, synchronically and diachronically, wide and deep. It gathers people together while maintaining a respectful distance – or at least ensuring that we do not fall over each other.

The analysis on which this study is based shades in a third semantic layering to Arendt's portraiture of 'the public': its fledgling quality. There is something inherently vulnerable about the public sphere, for all its openness and commonality. Nussbaum(1986) has written about 'the fragility of goodness', particularly in relation to the literature of nascent European democracy. The public sphere as democratically constructed is easily destabilized; it is fragile by nature; its composure is always at risk. On the one hand it is subject to the individual and competing interests of those who comprise it – creeping privatization; on the other hand, it is subject to corporate diktat and take-over – the new public management. It is a distinctly wobbly table that comprises this 'in between' of the public space: the *polis*, the *res publica*, the commonality by which and around which we co-exist.

That is the nature of the public sphere. Its sustainability resides in its necessary fragility: it comprises and reaches out to differences that render it inherently vulnerable. Its strength lies in that vulnerability, but that vulnerability also offers a sense of possibility. The polity is always at risk: from fundamentalists and those who are sure of certain certainties; but, also, from sceptics, cynics and scoffers; and from those who simply have no care for the world. Whatever is public and civic in us, as individuals, is always fledgling; always in the making and highly vulnerable; and always, therefore, costly. We share, as a polity, in the economic cost of the public good, just as we should also share in the social capital that accrues from that investment. A sense of reality must incorporate a sense of possibility: an investment of the resources of hope in the well being and sustainability of the future.

Civil Society

Unlike private association, civic association tends to be inclusive *in this sense that it is open in principle to anyone.*

(*Young, 2000, 161*)

The places of the polity are its institutions. When nation states fall apart, break down, become ungovernable, the process of recovery invariably begins with civic regeneration: with the recovery of locality, habitude and place. Under such circumstances, the resumption of institutional association and membership becomes the prime concern. States and societies exist by virtue of that institutional and associative middle ground, without which nation states lack legitimacy and societies lack cohesion. Institutions, at best, operate against tribalism, nepotism and other forms of exclusivity. They aim at civic engagement, participation and a sense of membership: what Young, quoted above, calls 'civic association . . . open in principle to anyone'.

However, that sense of institutional membership is invariably premised upon certain conditions or requirements: heritage, belief, common interest and/or purpose, adherence to rules, prior qualifications and/or experience, etc. Each is more or less exclusive, in respect of its conditions and requirements. Some churches are broad, others less so; some tents are big, some are decidedly cramped; some rainbows claim a wide spectrum of coalition, others a more modest spectral slice. None is entirely inclusive; most exact an 'admission charge' of some kind or other (confirmation, initiation, etc.); some demand an 'exit fee' of sorts (guilt, apostasy, etc.)

From the inside, then, institutions may feel inclusive, but from the outside they can be seen as exclusive and excluding. Since they invariably rely on overt or covert hierarchies or gradations of seniority, they may for some of those on the inside also feel less than inclusive. They may, therefore, from both within and without arouse the very sense of alienation that they seek to ameliorate through mutuality and a sense of belonging. The ostensible purpose of institutions is to conceive and construct a commonality. The problem is that commonalities involve common interests and that there are invariably some interests that are excluded, or considered to be excluded, from the commonality. If I can't play chess it may be difficult for me to be a member of the chess club.

Institutions may draw the line definitively and unambiguously through, for example, formal oath-taking or swearing-in ceremonies. For such institutions the key question is: *are you for us or against us?* Sometimes institutions may be drawn into a protracted internal debate as to where exactly the line should be drawn with regard to who's in and who's out. For these institutions the crucial question is one of institutional identity: *who are we?* Each of these 'types' requires different modes of institutional leadership: the former more often than not giving rise to charismatic styles of leadership and the latter to negotiative and persuasive styles of leadership. Problems occur when, as is often the case, the broad membership of the institution differs as to what kind of institution it constitutes and what kind of leadership it requires. (The 'Anglican communion', as it calls itself, is paradigmatic of this broad church – big tent – problem.)

Both these institutional 'types' look *inwards* for some measure of self definition. A third and perhaps increasingly significant 'type' of institution extends both the terms and the constituency of the debate as to where the line, or lines, should be drawn by reaching *outwards*. Here the key question is: *how might we best work for you?* These institutions deliberately place themselves on the edge and invite engagement. They neither fully know themselves nor fully understand their constituencies, but they do have a strong sense that their understanding of the latter and their knowledge of the former are inter-dependant. They are sure that, to survive as institutions, they have to open up a debate across the broader public sphere of civil society as to what membership and engagement mean. They assume that this debate cannot be conducted entirely from within: 'activities with a civic purpose', as Young (2000, 161) puts it, 'aim to serve not only members, but also the wider community'; they 'claim to make some contribution to the collective life of the neighbourhood, city, country, or the world'.

Institutions of higher education usually include elements from each of these 'types'. They have their own initiation ceremonies and regalia (inaugurals, gowns, insignias, etc.) and their own highly differentiated hierarchies of status (old, red brick, new, etc.). They also have a tradition of internal debate as to what they are there for and what precisely the 'idea of the university' might be. Increasingly, however, they are (or are being required to) define themselves in terms of the public interest: research is increasingly being justified and its quality judged with reference to, among other things, its impact on and relevance to its users; teaching programmes are increasingly justified in terms of their relevance in respect of student need and their quality judged with reference to feedback routinely provided by students; the service dimension of higher education provision is also increasingly open to public scrutiny and comment.

Within the higher education community this shift is sometimes viewed in negative terms. This negative response is understandable given the appallingly inept bureaucratic mechanisms of the accountability regimes with which it is associated. Nevertheless, recourse to notions of academic freedom and academic autonomy is a sloppy and inadequate response to the big idea that institutions of higher education need to redefine themselves within the public sphere and with reference to the broad public interest. Widening access to and participation in higher education is premised on that idea. The broadening of the educational franchise necessarily involves educational change. That is the implicit bargain: if society is to move rapidly towards a more educated citizenry, then the institutions of education must change radically. Higher education must, in short, reach beyond the confines of its own institutional and sector boundaries in order to gain legitimacy and credibility.

This emergent 'type' of institution (which is by no means restricted to the higher education sector) requires a new kind of academic practitioner and a new kind of academic leadership. These are the new 'liminal' professionals who are to be found in a wide range of institutional contexts: those who define their professionalism in terms of their cross-boundary knowledge and understanding, their ability to communicate, persuade and negotiate across multiple and sometimes ill-defined or fuzzy boundaries, and their orientation towards the recognition of difference. Within the higher education sector we no longer require those who are adept at boundary maintenance, but those who are committed to boundary transgression. We need to render the boundaries increasingly permeable.

Institutions of higher education are ideally placed within civil society to model and think through the implications of this emergent institutional practice: their research and scholarship is international in outreach; they recruit students from across the globe; they exchange information and ideas at international conferences and colloquia; they focus on topics such as 'globalization', 'international relations' and 'world affairs' in their teaching and research programmes. Institutions of higher education – universities – are by definition, and in practice, universal. Funding regimes based on fierce competition for limited research resources and student placements arguably make them less so, by forcing them to protect their own vested interests. Nevertheless their impulse – their moral compass – is towards what lies beyond their own institutional horizons.

Civic Engagement

And what lasts, what enters into our being as a result of school and college, is a blend of value, attitude and assumption, a certain moral tone, a special quality of imagination, a particular flavour of sensibility – the things that constituted the soul of our education.

(*Walsh, 1959, 54*)

Institutions of higher education are, then, one of the institutional places within the space of civil society to which we might look for civic regeneration.

They are one of the places, in other words, in which people gain a sense of their own unique 'blend of value, attitude and assumption', as Walsh (quoted above) puts it – and, in so doing, begin to make complicated connections, gain a critical understanding of what constitutes membership and belongingness, and learn what it means to be an independent learner reliant on interdependency as a crucial intellectual resource. They are the places where people 'go public' by, for example: writing essays and assignments; asking and responding to questions, presenting their own and others' viewpoints; talking about ideas; taking a principled stance; organizing all manner of events; representing particular staff or student constituencies. They are places of learning precisely because they offer, encourage and provide the institutional conditions necessary for these forms of imaginative engagement – the places that continue to constitute 'the soul of our education'.

Only insofar as institutions of higher education do indeed offer, encourage and provide those institutional conditions can they be said to be universities. Universities are at best places where people find a voice, a presence; where people participate and become citizens; where they discover the resources of leadership and purposefulness. Partisanship of any kind is alien to the idea of the university. The legitimacy of any institution of higher education cannot be premised on prior assumptions regarding the provenance of truth: truth as revealed through scripture, political party, or ideological orthodoxy. Higher education stands against the dictates of faith, political partisanship and intellectual fashion. It is the place where secular society reflects upon itself and on the basis of that reflection moves forward with confidence. It is the place where arguments are held open and where divergence of opinion and viewpoint is valued.

It is, however, in these places of learning that people discover how to take a stand, argue a particular point of view, listen to counter arguments, debate till midnight and discuss till dawn. These are the places, in other words, where people are provided with some of the capabilities necessary to become citizens. People can and do acquire these capabilities without higher education, but for those who take this route higher education is the institutional context within which they go some of the way towards discovering civic presence, civic participation and civic purpose. Higher education fails if it does not at least orientate its members – staff and students – towards this ideal of civic engagement.

That, of course, is the ideal. The reality is all too often rather different. Many students feel disenchanted. They point to a lack of personal contact with their tutors and to inadequate feedback. A significant proportion of students although nominally full time are virtually part time given the necessity to take paid work to fund their studies. Many academics feel stressed and under-valued. They point to widening pay differentials, lack of professional recognition and unremitting demands for bureaucratic accountability. They highlight the constant surveillance that characterizes their working lives. To acknowledge this reality is not, however, to disparage the ideal. Indeed, unless the ideal is upheld, there can be little hope of it ever being realized. It is important, therefore, to remind ourselves of the civic purpose of higher education as an essential element within civil society.

Education and voice: civic presence

Higher education should provide its students with the capabilities necessary to find a voice and a presence within the polity: empowered citizens, not token citizens; active citizens, not loyal subjects (see Phillips, 1995). In finding that voice they learn not to be opinionated, but to hold informed opinions and to communicate these opinions with sensitivity to the wider context of ideas within which the opinions originated. Civic presence is consequent upon the acquisition of that voice. Without an informed articulacy and a sense of rightful place within the polity, students cannot gain a sense of civic presence. Learning how to read and write – learning how to learn – is a deeply political process. Hermeneutics and politics are, both philosophically and practically, closely aligned.

A sense of civic presence emerges from and is sustained by what is known. As the horizon of what is known extends, so does the mind of the knower. The world becomes knowable. Still sometimes strange, alienating, 'out there', uncertain, the world nevertheless through the pursuit of knowledge and understanding begins to be governable. It becomes a book that can be read, interpreted and re-read. It becomes open to translation. It may remain a difficult and in some ways even an opaque text, but now nevertheless it is becoming a text: to be received and understood, argued over and critiqued, discussed and debated. In this complicated process – which is, crucially, an *educational* process – people begin to take responsibility for their own lives and for their own trajectories.

Our civic presence in the world is dependent therefore upon our gaining the capabilities necessary to read the text of the world: to distinguish between an atoll and an aphid; to trace the sometimes hidden link between words and things; to find our own way through the mind-maze. That maze constitutes our world of things, people, fabrications, matter, words, meanings, ideas, etc., all of which have to be interpreted and understood by those who live in and take forward the world. In helping take it forward into the unknown and largely unknowable future, we share responsibility for it. The future is ours insofar as we discover, and are given the conditions necessary to discover, our own voices and our own presences in the world. Without that heuristic drive towards discovery – and the conditions necessary for discovery – subjects cannot claim their right to citizenship.

Education and citizenship: civic participation

Citizenship requires participation in the polity and that polity requires an informed citizenry with the capabilities necessary to (1) deliberate together on the ends and purposes of the good society (2) recognize and respect value differences regarding what constitutes right action in particular circumstances and (3) in the light of those deliberations and understandings move towards albeit provisional and amendable agreements as to how best they can live together. Central to the notion of civic participation are those three big ideas: deliberation (as thinking together about right action), recognition (as respect for difference) and agreement-making (as a complex and ongoing democratic process) No person can be a citizen on her or his own. Citizens require a citizenry in order to be able to think and act as citizens.

Undemocratic regimes know this all too well. That is why their first response to those citizens who have the courage to argue for their own and others' citizenly rights is to isolate them: through house arrest, imprisonment, allegations of disloyalty to the state, the suppression of minority or indigenous languages, separation from family and support groups, 'disappearance', etc. In this they eventually and inevitably fail because a democratic citizenry has allegiances beyond the regulatory mechanisms of the nation state: both inwards to older traditions and structures of cooperation and solidarity; outwards to new and emergent social formations and movements pressing for change; and sideways to new civic coalitions and alliances. The global and international dimensions of citizenship – of reaching out to wider constituencies and communities – are becoming increasingly important.

To take but one example: the Burmese ruling party cannot silence Aung San Suu Kyi (pro-democracy activist and leader of the National League of Democracy in Burma). They cannot do so, because she knows something that its leaders do not know: namely, that politics is about power not force; that whenever the powerful resort to force, their political legitimacy is diminished; and that power is generated by the political will of people thinking together, acting together and recognizing how difficult thinking together and acting together are in a world of difference. She knows that the people of Burma are strong and fast not because in 1989 a military junta officially renamed their country 'Myanmar' (Burmese for 'strong and fast') but because they are the people of Burma.

Citizens are not just persons who exercise independent agency. They are agents who are determined to act *together* in recognition of their differences as well as their commonalities. They assume that, individually, there is a lot they cannot know (and cannot know that they do not know); that collectively there might be significantly less that they do not know (and a greater chance of knowing what it is that they do not know); and that action based on shared knowledge and understanding is, therefore, more likely to recognize and be responsive to divergent interests, needs and wants. Deliberative democracy does not simply guarantee that there are more bits and pieces of knowledge and understanding to add to the communal pool. It also serves to provide checks and balances against modes of thinking that assume the problems and challenges are self-evident, the answers and solutions straightforward and the implications unproblematic.

Education and leadership: civic purpose

Intellectual leadership in the context of civic participation means, therefore, keeping open the long deliberative process of argumentation beyond the point of seemingly irreconcilable difference. Superficial consensus is relatively easy to achieve provided that differences are kept to a minimum and inconvenient disagreements are conveniently sidelined. Deep agreements that recognize diverse and even conflicting individual and community interests – and hold open the long argument regarding the ends and purposes of the good society and the means of achieving those ends and purposes – are much more difficult to achieve. Leaders are all too often judged on the basis of their ability to do things right, rather than to work towards a situation in which all involved are agreed on what are the right things to do. That is precisely the point at which leaders become managers, managers become micro-managers, and the micro-managers become operatives: the point, that is, at which intellectual leadership is lost.

Across the higher education sector intellectual leadership is in short supply. Leadership usually means protecting the vested interests of a particular institution or institutional bloc. That is how the pecking-order of pro vice chancellors and vice chancellors is determined and how salaries are decided behind closed doors across the sector: not what is in the best interests of the sector as a whole or indeed the education system as a whole, but what best places this particular institution to win over its rivals. Policies justified on the grounds of institutional diversity and student choice in reality serve to usher in a system of institutional inequality and a diminution of student choice. An increasingly differentiated student fee structure coupled with an unequal distribution of research funding across institutions and subjects does not equate with the ends and purposes of a just society.

On the contrary it equates with what Toynbee and Walker (2009, 71), two leading political and social commentators within the UK, term 'unjust rewards': the fact that '7% of private-school children take 45% of Oxbridge places and these pupils are five times more likely than state-school leavers to be offered a place in a top Russell Group University'. They suggest: 'For the privileged the dice are loaded ever more heavily. Top universities will continue to under-represent the majority of students whose parents don't or can't pay for their education' (p. 74). This systemic problem of increasing social inequality points less to leadership based on a sense of civic purpose than to the management of institutional self-interest: or, as Toynbee and Walker put it, to an ongoing and still largely unchallenged policy of 'unjust rewards'. Any such policy is to the detriment of society as a whole, since, as Wilkinson and Pickett (2009) persuasively argue, 'more equal societies almost always do better' just as more unequal societies almost always do worse. The 'spirit level' of society, to employ their metaphor, needs to show a levelling out of inequalities and an increasingly even distribution of social and economic well being across society. (See also Patel, 2009.)

Towards an Ethics of Hospitality

Citizenship is given expression in the arena of public discourse.
(Ranson and Stewart, 1994, 249)

Derrida (2001, 16–18) identifies the ethical dimension of the civic with what he calls 'hospitality'. Indeed, he argues that the phrase 'ethic of hospitality' is 'tautologous'. So thoroughly coextensive is hospitality with the experience of hospitality that *'ethics is hospitality'* (original emphasis). Recalling Dante ('banished from Florence and then welcomed, it would seem, at Ravenna') he begins to trace the genealogy of 'hospitality' in relation to 'the city'. In the medieval tradition one can identify what he calls 'a certain sovereignty of the city', so that

> the city itself could determine the laws of hospitality, the articles of pre-determined law, both plural and restrictive, with which they meant to condition the Great Law of Hospitality – an unconditional Law, both singular and universal, which ordered that the borders be open to each and every one, to every other, to all who might come, without question or without their even having to identify who they are or whence they came.

The argument is, as always with Derrida, working hard on a lot of fronts: not least of which is the implied comparison between what he calls 'the Great Law of Hospitality' and much current legislation relating to the treatment and status of cross-border refugees (which is far from hospitable). He argues that the civic virtues necessarily inflect towards the hospitable. If the social sphere requires and is conditional upon an ethics of recognition, then the civic sphere is premised on an ethics of hospitality. To develop as a citizen is to learn how to be hospitable: how to be open and receptive to others; how to practise civic engagement as inclusion; how to see boundaries as permeable and negotiable. The civic is an open space in which we learn how to be open. It is, as Ranson and Stewart quoted above point out, the arena of public discourse in which citizenship is given expression.

The place of the university within that space is crucial. It is partly a question of how higher education can itself become more inclusive and open; partly a question of how higher education can assist in the formation of an educated and sophisticated citizenry open to divergence and plurality; and partly a matter of how universities envisage their purpose within civil society. The purpose of higher education has tended to be viewed through a fairly narrow lens of institutional 'efficiency', 'performativity' and 'cost-effectiveness'; and that, in turn, makes it all the more difficult to identify and develop higher education practices that are inclusive and open and that encourage participants to think critically about notions of citizenship and citizenry. Seddon's (2008) analysis is particularly important in this respect, relating as it does to notions of 'civic formation' and what she terms 'transforming politics'.

Seddon's starting point, although not easily categorizable as 'Marxist', is located in the Marxist cannon. Quoting from Marx and Engels (1976) *German Ideology*, she argues that an alternative starting point does not set out 'from what men [sic] say, imagine, conceive, nor from men as narrated, thought of, imagined, conceived, in order to arrive at men in the flesh; but

[sets] out from real, active men, and . . . their real life processes' (Marx and Engels, 1976, 42, quoted in Seddon, 2008, 155). She sees this as a 'transforming politics' located in the 'ever-moving present': 'overemphasizing the impact of the past forgets that people change circumstances in their present everyday circumstances. And in this recurring present there is no guide to the future' (p. 156). The educator must educate herself in the 'ever-moving present'. That is the only way in which she can face and enable others to face a necessarily unforeseeable future.

From this starting point Seddon argues that 'active citizenship [is] something that is done in everyday local places, which are also spaces shaped by people of mobility, global horizons, cultural difference and reflexive engagement'. This 'citizen action', as she calls it, 'is framed by everyday discourses and their assumptions about belonging and learning, individual and collective benefit'. Civic engagement, in other words, is 'a practice lived through harmonization and history in highly contextualised ways' (p.161). It is not an abstracted ideal, but a lived reality: a practice embedded in real lives located in real histories and real places.

Seddon explains this lived reality in terms of an axis of 'belonging' and 'learning' and an intersecting axis of 'collectivized benefits' and 'individual benefits'. Belonging as a collectivized benefit requires according to this schema the practice of social activism, while learning as a collectivized benefit requires the practice of community building. Belonging and learning are transformed into permeable and inclusive categories, as opposed to exclusive or individualistic categories, by becoming collectivized benefits. The citizenry to which each of us belongs, and the learning from which each of us benefits, includes and is immeasurably enhanced by the inclusion of the other. That is the ethics of hospitality. (See Table 3.1.)

What that ethics of hospitality means in practice is a matter of how students are conceptualized as a body politic, how institutions of higher education are conceived as being at the heart of civil society, and how civil society is seen as being integral to the semantics of a 'language of deliberative democracy' (see Nixon, 2004). These are not technical matters that

Table 3.1   Practices of civic engagement

	Belonging	Learning
Collectivized benefits	Social activist	Community builder
Individual benefits	Individual learner	'Can-Do' innovator

Adapted from Seddon (2008, 161).

can be addressed in a 'how to do it' format. They confront the awkward question, as Dahrendorf (1994) poses it: 'can we survive in freedom?' Or as Touraine (2000), with perhaps more simplistic flair puts it: 'can we live together?' There are no easy answers to these questions, but Habermas (1994, 32) provides a helpful pointer in highlighting the need for 'a kind of communicative pluralism' based on the premise that 'an inclusive public sphere cannot be organised as a whole; it depends rather on the stabilizing context of a liberal and egalitarian political culture': the public sphere as a kind of loose federation of collectivized interests and benefits.

That, of course, complicates the problem enormously. If the public sphere comprises a plurality of publics, then how can belonging and learning be inclusive and how can benefits be collectivized? Do we not slip back to the substratum of individual benefits which privileges individual learners and 'can-do' innovators? Does not the public sphere implode into fragmented mini-spheres of competing self-interest: the Hobbesian nightmare? That is the point at which an ethics of hospitality (as elaborated in this chapter) confronts an ethics of recognition (as elaborated in the previous chapter); and, crucially, how these two ethical frameworks square up to an ethics of magnanimity (as discussed towards the end of the following chapter).

What is clear is that we in the supposedly developed Western world have got it badly wrong – ethically. As a result, poor social and economic policy has ensued. We have failed to see how rising income and consumption for individuals impacts upon collective social and economic improve-ment: how, for example, increasing disparities in financial remuneration, far from having a beneficial drip-down effect on the less well off, have a malign effect on society as a whole. The public is now picking up the tab for, at best, the irresponsibility of the private sector and, at worst, its prof-ligacy. ('Proflicacy' may be the appropriate term when one bears in mind that in a single year a FTSE-100 executive could earn what it would take an employee working a 40-hour week on the minimum wage 226 years to earn.) The basis of policy aimed at the public good is that it maximizes – not economic growth, personal incomes and consumption for individuals – but the widening of opportunities for all through collective action and deliberative decision-making.

Hobsbawm (2009), still the conscience and memory of an older leftist orientation, sums up the situation in Britain in the following character-istically uncompromising terms: 'Britain deregulated its markets, sold its industries to the highest bidder, stopped making things to export . . . and put its money on becoming the global centre of financial services and therefore a paradise for zillionaire money launderers'. That's the bad ethics – the failure of public policy. What follows are the implications of that failure – a fractured polity: 'that is why the impact of the world crisis on the pound and the British economy today is likely to be more catastrophic than on any other major Western economy – and that full recovery may well be harder'. Increasing inequalities and the erosion of collective social improvement make neither economic nor ethical sense, as Hobsbawm, driving the point home, makes clear: 'inadequate schools are not offset by the fact that London universities could field a football team of Nobel prize winners'.

***

Our identity as citizens is premised on our social identity, just as our being human is premised on our social being. Were we not social we would not be human; were we not citizens we would not be social; being social is intrinsic to our human being and provides the basis of our becoming citizens. This set of ontological connections and relations is central to the argument: to be human is to be social and to be social is to be civic, and to be civic is to extend our humanity into the public domain of collective action and improvement. This process of human flourishing and development is itself *educative* – education, to evoke Williams (1989, 14) again, is 'ordinary', precisely because it is grounded in our common humanity and our shared practices. Starting from (Stiglitz's 2002, 20) assumption that 'globalization itself is neither good nor bad . . . [but] has the *power* to do enormous good' (original emphasis), Chapter 4 sets the argument as developed in this and the previous chapter within the broader debate on globalization, cosmopolitanism and the possibility of cosmopolitan learning.

Chapter 4

Cosmopolitan Imaginaries

The important fact now is that the human condition has itself become cosmopolitan.

(Beck, 2006, 2)

Cosmopolitanism is a highly contested term. In this chapter I distinguish between, on the one hand, a dominant 'neoliberal' or 'corporate' version of market-led globalization and, on the other, an emergent and still fragile democratically inflected cosmopolitanism. The former, as Gamble (2000, 91) puts it, 'vigorously attacks all notions of the public good, of public altruism, of enlightened paternalism, or neutral and omniscient government'. Rooted in the assumption 'that concepts such as the public interest and enlightened government or government for the good of the people have no meaning' (p. 90), it enjoys the unreserved support of the public choice wing of neoliberalism. The latter is rooted in a very different set of assumptions. Within this alternative version the local is not subsumed by the global. Rather, each is understood with reference to the other within a context of open regionalism. This is a cosmopolitanism that is deeply relational at various interconnected levels: the local, the regional, the national, the international and the global. It is this alternative version, which, although as yet emergent and fledgling, provides us with a cosmopolitan imaginary.

Beck (2006, 2) suggests the cosmopolitan human condition is now not only a fact, but an 'important fact' that is itself constitutive of the human condition. The analysis developed in this chapter suggests that this 'important fact' of the changing nature of the human condition – of what might be characterized as an emergent democratic cosmopolitanism – must be understood in its imaginary potential. The 'important fact' has, in other words, to be imagined into being. Whatever cosmopolitan learning might mean, it undoubtedly involves our understanding of ourselves and others in a world of difference – and, crucially, in relation to one another and to each other. Relationality is central to the notion of cosmopolitan imaginaries as developed within the argument of this book.

The public space is a space within which we necessarily belong. Belongingness matters. The questions posed in this chapter relate centrally to this notion of belongingness: how might higher education enhance a sense of belongingness? How might higher education encourage a sense of belongingness within the wider global society? How might higher education enable students to feel a sense of institutional affiliation and association while belonging to a wider international community? What might 'cosmopolitan learning' (learning within and for a democratic *cosmopolity*) mean within the context of a deeply stratified higher education sector? The human condition may indeed have become cosmopolitan, but that condition has to be understood, worked through, thought through and developed in terms of its implications for human well being and fulfilment.

It has, in other words, to be understood educationally. The educational mediation of an, as yet, emergent democratically inflected *cosmopolis* is the major theme of this chapter. Where and how we are located globally affects who we are, what and how we know ourselves and others, and how we conceptualize our ends and purposes. Only when the *cosmopolity* is understood ontologically, epistemologically and teleologically can its democratic potential begin to be realized. The task is not simply to read off certain educational implications and consequences against the fact (and brute force) of globalization, but to read into globalization new educational possibilities (of understanding and imagination) that speak back to the seeming inevitability of that brute force. Tracing the trajectory of the cosmopolitan imaginary is an educational process, the hermeneutical endpoint of which is to understand ourselves and one another in relation to each other.

The *Cosmopolis*

Cosmopolis is not only a utopia but a nightmare, too.

(Archibugi, 2002, 37)

How we conceptualize the *cosmopolis* depends very much on the particular version of cosmopolitanism that we choose to employ; and whether, as Archibugi puts it, we see it as a utopia or a nightmare – or, perhaps, a realizable and worthwhile aspiration. Of course, one person's utopia may be another person's nightmare, just as one person's realizable and worthwhile aspiration may, for another, be wholly unrealizable and/or not particularly worthwhile. Since this chapter is premised on the view that implicit in education are, as Rizvi (2008) puts it, 'cosmopolitan possibilities' and that these possibilities are both worthwhile educationally and educationally realizable, then we need to examine some of the tensions and contradictions inherent in this highly contested notion of the *cosmopolis*.

The dominant version has been variously described as 'neoliberal cosmopolitanism' (Gowan, 2001), 'the new imperialism' (Archibugi, 2002), and 'corporate cosmopolitanism' (Rizvi, 2009). It might be characterized as the cosmopolitanism of the international elite intent upon colonizing an ever expanding 'neoliberalizing space' of privatization and deregulation, competition and economic efficiency, and freedom of individual choice (Peck and Tickle, 2002). The idea of cosmopolitanism based on these neoliberal and corporatist principles, argues Rizvi (2009, 259), 'suggests that the market, as a single global sphere of free trade, has the potential to promote greater intercultural understanding and peace'. It thereby 'assumes the self-regulative capacity of the market and takes all human beings as equal potential trading partners' – or, as Gowan (2001, 79) puts it with more than a hint of irony, this 'new liberal cosmopolitanism' envisages 'a single human race peacefully united by free trade and common legal norms, led by states featuring civic liberties and representative institutions'.

This 'new liberal cosmopolitanism' – appealing though it may be to the global elite with the financial and social capital necessary to translate their ideal of individual freedom of choice into a material reality – is not without its flaws. First, the notion of individuality upon which it is based assumes a particular kind of inter-subjectivity: 'it valorizes cosmopolitan subjects who are culturally flexible and adaptable who are able to take advantage of the global processes that paradoxically are portrayed as objective and historically inevitable' (Rizvi, 2009, 260). The supposed freedom of the 'culturally flexible and adaptable' individual is, in other words, illusory: the supposedly 'objective and historically inevitable' global processes to which we are encouraged to adapt by way of historical necessity are deeply subjective (in the sense of being incorporated into our emotions and preferences) and historically determinate (in the sense of being within our own determination).

The second point follows from the first as night follows day: the 'new liberal cosmopolitanism' masks the persistent and growing inequalities within and across societies. These inequalities are both structural and systemic, but are also part of consciousness and everyday life (see Calhoun, 2002; Ray, 2007). Indeed, it is precisely because inequalities are internalized in this way – as part of the taken-for-granted, 'given', and 'natural' order of life as we live it – that they become structurally and systemically embedded within the social order. The 'new liberal cosmopolitanism' presupposes, against the evidence of every 'spirit level' of economic and social well being available, a level plane of global transactions upon which individuals compete on merit and exercise their unrestrained freedom of choice (Wilkinson and Pickett, 2009). This version of cosmopolitanism mystifies and romanticizes – and conversely demonizes – those who do not live up to the romantic ideal of neo-liberal freedom.

The third flaw of this version of cosmopolitanism is what Appiah (2006) highlights as its universalism: its assumption that one set of global relations and loyalties (e.g. the global market) necessarily overrides other sets of local, regional and national relations and loyalties (e.g. patriotism). Cosmopolitanism thereby becomes a kind of absolutism, in relation to which local affiliation, community association and love of place and country become subsidiary. My multiple identities (rooted in extended family, occupation, locality, country, etc.) become consumed by that of an abstract and un-localized single identity (rootless, transitional and in perpetual motion). This, to draw on Sen's (2007) analysis, is a kind of 'violence': the violence inflicted by a notion of identity as singular and monolithic on specific identities that are necessarily pluralist, relational and historically and geo-politically located.

An alternative and emergent version of democratic cosmopolitanism has to be imagined *against* the dominant version of 'neoliberal' or 'corporate' cosmopolitanism. This imaginary has a complex trajectory expressed in part as an aspiration towards new forms of global governance and interconnectivity and in part as an impulse towards new cultural formations of identity and difference and new social solidarities of value. The 'cosmopolitan possibilities' of education have to be understood in the context of this dynamic process of transformation: a dialectical process whereby agency is increasingly defined in and through the emergent structures of global governance, which are in turn shaped by the actions and understandings of the participating agents. This dialectic is not an outcome of, but is constitutive of, the *cosmopolis* conceived as an ongoing struggle for democratic participation.

Archibugi (2000, 144) employs the term 'cosmopolitical democracy' in order to highlight the political significance of this struggle: 'what distinguishes cosmopolitical democracy from other such projects is its attempt to create institutions which enable the voice of individuals to be heard in global affairs, irrespective of their resonance at home'. Democracy is layered in such a way that the *polity* and the *cosmopolity* are seen as mutually sustaining – 'a form of global governance' that needs to be realized on 'three different, interconnected levels: within states, between states, and at a world level'. That set of distinctions leads to the big question that lies at the heart of Archibugi's argument: 'Why shouldn't the process of democracy – which has already had to overcome a thousand obstacles within individual states – assert itself beyond national borders, when every other aspect of human life today, from economy to culture, from sport to social life, has a global dimension?' (Archibugi, 2000, 147)

Gorbachev (2009), writing as former leader of the Soviet Union (1985–1991) and current president of the World Political Forum, sees this kind of organic linkage as central to what he refers to as 'New Thinking': 'the organic linkage between changes in the economic, technological, social, demographic and cultural conditions that determine the daily existence of billions of people on our planet'. The global economic crisis has shown that 'not only bureaucratic socialism but also ultra-liberal capitalism are in need of profound democratic reform – their own kind of perestroika'. A flawed model (and ideology) of Soviet-style economic planning cannot simply be replaced by what is now acknowledged to be a flawed model (and ideology) of Western-style capitalism. A new mindset is required whereby 'we can think of ourselves as active participants in the process of creating a new world'. (For the origins of the 'New Thinking' in the events of 1989, see: Engel, 2009; Pleshakov, 2009; Sebestyen, 2009. For an overview of the recent and relevant literature on 1989, see: Garton Ash, 2009a; 2009b)

What is being imagined here is a global civil society that recognizes the sovereignty of the state, the mandate of inter-state alliances, and the possibility of forms of governance and accountability agreed and applied worldwide; a society in which citizens have opportunities to participate directly in making global choices and to applying the principles of democracy internationally. (Archibugi, 2008; Cabrera, 2004). The emphasis within this cosmopolitan imaginary is on what Cohen (1997) calls the 'new diasporas', on new social movements and emergent cultural communities, on disenfranchised and minority groups: 'to respond to the challenges facing us today we have to reconstruct democracy, with an effort of the imagination analogous to that of the eighteenth-century passages from direct to representative forms' (Archibugi, 2002, 29). That 'effort of the imagination', as conceived by Archibugi, is necessarily an *educational* effort: an effort, that is, of interpretive enquiry, of critical understanding and awareness, and of thinking across and beyond given boundaries.

Global Contexts

Why do stakeholders in higher education world-wide – governors, institutions, including staff and students, and community, including business and industry – seek to internationalize universities?

(Blight, Davis and Olsen, 2000, 101)

There is no simple answer to the question posed above. Education in general and higher education in particular are central to the imaginative reconstruction of cosmopolitan society, since what are being reconstructed are our own understandings and our own awareness of what democratic participation means within a global context. The political transformation involved in the making of cosmopolitan democracy is necessarily an ethical and educational transformation. Part of the answer to the question posed above is to be found, therefore, in Archibugi's vision of 'cosmopolitical democracy' and in the need to ensure that this vision is understood both ethically and educationally. It also, however, has to be understood within the global context of what Brennan (2001, 77) refers to as the 'contemporary neo-liberal orthodoxy': the complex and shifting nexus of market forces and the ideology that informs it. Viewed from this perspective, institutions of higher education are located within a global and highly competitive market. If stakeholders in higher education world-wide seek to internationalize universities, that is in part at least because higher education is a big and burgeoning international business.

Indeed, it is *very* big business. Income from non-EU students is crucial to UK institutions of higher education because they bring in income that is not conditional upon UK government support. 'Internationalization', as Harris (2007, 128) puts it, 'matters in the contemporary university because money is crucial, and universities can increase their incomes substantially through the high fees charged to international students'. Home UK and EU students pay tuition fees which fall well below the full economic costing of the courses on which they are enrolled and is supplemented by the government through public expenditure. Places for home UK and EU students are therefore limited – or 'capped' to use the terminology. Non-EU international students provide, on the other hand, an open and much more lucrative market, with some such students paying more than £20,000 a year in fees alone. From the point of view of the university and indeed the government, non-EU international student recruitment is not only an attractive option but a financial necessity.

To put this in perspective, it has been estimated that in 2007–2008 £1.88 billion of UK universities' income came from non-EU students, while £1.76 billion came from government research grants. Given the financial implications of non-EU student recruitment, it is hardly surprising that there has been a sharp increase in that area of recruitment over the last ten years. One in ten enrolments in 2007–2008 – 229,640 students – was from outside the EU. In 1998–1999, the figure was 117,290, which makes the increase 96%. China has continued to be the most significant provider of students to UK higher education across most levels of study. India and Nigeria feature strongly among taught higher degree students, while students from the United States and the countries of the Middle East and South Asia (India, Pakistan, Saudi Arabia, Iran, Libya and Egypt) are prominent among research postgraduates. At a time of financial pressure, international non-EU student income is enabling universities to survive and in some cases to invest and expand. (See Universities UK, 2009.)

The reliance on these markets is not, however, without its risks. The markets shift significantly and sometimes rapidly depending upon the global economy and the economic and educational needs of particular geographical areas. Courses that are sustained by overseas students primarily drawn from one locale may find themselves facing drastic reduction in numbers over a relatively short space of time because of factors that are beyond their control. While a large fee income from non-EU students may render universities sustainable, it also makes them vulnerable precisely because they are heavily reliant on this largely unpredictable source of income. There is also the problem of ensuring excellence of service from the point of first enquiry, through arrival, induction and welfare, to course provision, graduation and follow-through support. Overseas recruitment relies heavily on goodwill and the continuing quality of all-through provision.

Again, some aspects of quality assurance may be outside the control of the institution. Changes to the visa system for student entry to the UK, as occurred in 2009, can, for example, seriously hamper universities' best intentions in creating an efficient system of entry and induction for students and in some cases their families. This change in the visa system had a particularly deleterious effect on potential students entering the UK from some of the main areas of overseas recruitment. In Pakistan alone – a major area of recruitment for research degree programmes – an estimated backlog of 14,000 applicants has caused major disruption for students who had been due to start courses in UK universities in 2009. As the president of Universities UK has put it, 'we are very concerned that significant numbers of students from Pakistan may not receive their visas in time to start their studies in the UK this year'. (See Williams and Shepherd, 2009.)

Notwithstanding these risks, the internationalization of higher education has contributed hugely to relations across national boundaries both at the institutional level and at the levels of policy development and interchange and of knowledge transfer. It has also contributed to the international reputation of UK higher education and, crucially, to its financial viability. The cosmopolitan possibilities of higher education cannot, however, be defined solely in terms of overseas student recruitment. They also have to be realized through a process of educational transformation: the realization of a new *cosmopolis*. The creation and sustainability of a new 'cosmopolitan democracy' has implications for both learning about our own selves and becoming other-wise. (See Odysseos, 2003.) These implications are deeply and inescapably educational.

Cosmopolitan Learning

I think the thing that makes me most proud, insofar as it is true, has been my effort to perceive what's going on in the world from a non-provincial perspective: to try to make sense of it from the angle of the great mass of the world's population . . . I think it is very important for young people to be shaken out of national prejudices and falsehoods. It's been a huge satisfaction to me that, in my work, I've been able to keep that going.

(Gowan, 2009, 69–70)

These thoughts were voiced by Peter Gowan, political activist, internationalist and academic, just months before he died – and as I was writing this book. (See Ali, 2009.) They remind us that cosmopolitanism as it relates to the practice of education is not some passing pedagogical fad. Nor is it restricted to courses relating specifically to international relations or targeted exclusively at overseas students. Given the reality of globalization, a cosmopolitan outlook is a necessary component of all higher education provision. The cosmopolitan possibilities of higher education originate in the realization that we are all living in a world that is becoming increasingly 'cosmopolitanized': a world characterized by what Beck (2006, 19) terms '*really existing cosmopolitanization*' (original emphasis).

Cosmopolitanism, argues Beck, is not a conscious and voluntary choice, but 'a function of coerced choices or a side effect of unconscious decisions'

(p. 19). Whether we like it or not we are all subject to this 'latent cosmopolitanism, *unconscious* cosmopolitanism, *passive* cosmopolitanism which shapes reality as side effects of global trade or global threats such as climate change, terrorism or financial crises' (original emphases) (p. 19). The cultivation of a cosmopolitan outlook – consciously and actively undertaken – is an educational necessity if we are to engage critically with *'really existing cosmopolitanization'*. This is the only way of transforming a 'latent cosmopolitanism' that is 'despotic' in its imposition of coerced choices into a 'realistic cosmopolitanism' that is 'emancipatory' in its public recognition of both the impact of this sustained coercion and the possibility of collective action premised on free choice (pp. 44–45). Connectivity, reflexivity and a developing sense of alternative futures are the moral and epistemological bases of this process of educational emancipation.

Education and relationality: cosmopolitan connectivity

Cosmopolitanism is not an appendix of the body politic, but is carried in the bloodstream. It shapes our relations one with another and informs the myriad connectivities that comprise *la vie commune*. Education for what Rizvi (2009, 263–267) calls 'cosmopolitan learning' is centrally concerned with understanding these connectivities with reference to specific cases and contexts: 'in developing such an understanding, education has a major role to play in helping students to realize that each experience of connectivity has a specific history from which it has emerged, and that global connectivity is a dynamic phenomenon, politically and historically changing – and that it is not only experienced differently, but is also interpreted differently in different contexts' (p. 263). The implications of this insight are far reaching at all levels: from inter-personal relationships to inter-state relations.

One wonders, for example, how the challenge of post-conflict economic and civic reconstruction in the Middle East might have been met had this lesson been taken to heart – and the histories and cultures of war-torn states thereby seen as part of the long-term solution rather than part of the ongoing problem. (See del Castillo, 2009.) Bombing such states back to the Dark Ages (as one of the US 'hawks' famously put it) would seem to be relatively easy; rebuilding them from the rubble is much more difficult. Indeed, the evidence would seem to suggest that there is very little collective understanding of how to re-establish local, regional and global connectivities when these have been deliberately and systematically destroyed – or even how to establish and develop them under more propitious circumstances.

'The problem', as Stiglitz (2006) puts it, 'is that economic globalization has outpaced the globalisation of politics and mindset'. The politics and the mindset are simply not available or at least is in short supply – which makes it all the more important that students are helped to understand that global connectivity is a dynamic phenomenon, politically and historically changing, and impacting on all our lives.

What does this emphasis on connectivity mean pedagogically? Rizvi suggests that 'cosmopolitan learning involves pedagogic tasks that help students explore the criss-crossing of transnational circuits of communication, the flows of global capital and the cross-cutting of local, translocal and transnational social practices' (p. 265). How, in other words, does *'really existing cosmopolitanization'* work at precise points and within specific sectors? Rizvi further suggests that 'such learning encourages students to consider the contested politics of place making, the social construction of power differentials and the dynamic processes relating to the formation of individual, group, national and transnational identities, and their corresponding fields of difference'. How, at those precise points and within those specific sectors, does relationality reinforce and resist the existing structures of power?

Education and identity: cosmopolitan reflexivity

Reality is becoming cosmopolitan – this, as Beck (2006, 68) puts it, is an 'historical fact'. Two questions then arise: 'how does the cosmopolitanization of reality become conscious?' and 'What conditions hinder or favour a collective awareness of really existing cosmopolitanism . . .?' One of the precise points upon which *'really existing cosmopolitanization'* impacts is, in other words, one's own identity – and that of others. Becoming aware of that impact and its consequences is central to 'cosmopolitan learning'. Without this reflexivity – this attempt to locate oneself and others within the processes one is seeking to understand – cosmopolitanism remains despotic: rendering us passive through its hidden influence on our choices, tastes and expectations. Cosmopolitanism only becomes emancipatory when we acknowledge its objective reality, locate ourselves inter-subjectively within that reality, and thereby achieve a critical awareness of the options available and of the alternative routes through.

To be reflexive is to be self-conscious and knowledgeable about one's own perspective – one's own cultural and political presuppositions – and how that perspective becomes open to change as a result of engaging with alternative perspectives and presuppositions. Reflexivity involves critically reflecting on one's own assumptions, some of which may be deeply ingrained and reinforced by communal loyalties and generally accepted norms. To be reflexive is to think against the grain of 'common sense' and to ask oneself the really awkward questions. To be reflexive regarding one's own position within *'really existing cosmopolitanization'* is to push this self questioning onto a different level – the level of 'cosmopolitan learning'. It is to locate oneself as a cosmopolitan learner within a pedagogical space of hugely expanded proportions.

Education is a process of formation – it helps form the identity of the learner through the development of understanding and expectation, the acquisition of knowledge and know-how, self awareness and awareness of the world. 'Cosmopolitan learning' contributes to this process through its emphasis on what Lingard (2008) refers to as the 'deparochializing' of pedagogies. 'Productive pedagogies', he argues, 'work with not against multiplicity' because they are rooted in 'a non-Eurocentric, non-sexist, reflexive critical humanism, stressing and respecting similarities as well as differences across all peoples and cultures' (p. 220). Viewed in this light, learning becomes, as Ranson (2008, 200) puts it, 'a reflexive expansion of capability, an enlarging of mutual mentality [which] embodies a journey in recognising the value of goods worth pursuing – especially those internal goods of reflexive evaluation that are valued because they enable us to judge the progress we are making in the activities which fill our collective lives.'

Education and transformation: cosmopolitan futures

Ranson concludes the above statement by asserting that the 'enlarging of mutual mentality . . . also involves a journey from our parochial particularity towards the understanding of the universal' (p. 200). That image of the ongoing (note the 'towards') journey captures something of the transformative potential of 'cosmopolitan learning'. The 'understanding of the universal' towards which the journey is directed cannot abandon the 'parochial particularity' which was its point of departure. The universal by definition is inclusive of the parochial, but locates it within a radically different hermeneutic. The parochial is now situated within the interpretive frame of the cosmopolitan outlook. That is how transformation works – not by forsaking one's origins, but by making of them a beginning through 'a reflexive expansion of capability' that opens up new possibilities and new futures.

Indeed, it is important to emphasize that transformation is always rooted in the local. It is always located and positioned. It happens in particular places, at precise points, within specific locales. As Berlin (1996, 22) pointed out, it is the specificity of what actually takes place that renders events trans-formative: 'the situation . . . as it occurred at the particular time, in the par-ticular place, as the result of the particular antecedents, in the framework of the particular events in which it and it alone occurred – the respects in which it differs from everything which has occurred before or is likely to occur after it'. A universality which loses this grasp of particularity loses its capacity for transformative change. The understanding of the universal must include a radical re-interpretation of the particular.

This means that transformation like education itself is a gradual process of realignment and readjustment, of shifting and rooting, of self-recogni-tion and the recognition of others. It is gradual because it is relational and because all social relations take time to develop. Although transformation may involve 'flashes of insight' and 'eureka moments', transformation itself is a process, not a one-off event. It happens in long time. Higher educa-tion, on the other hand, happens in organized time and within a fixed time frame. To be transformative the experience of higher education must build on the past educational experience of the learner and open up new possibilities for future learning. It must be integral to the learner's life nar-rative. Since, as Sennett (2006, 36) points out, 'a life narrative in which the individual matters to others requires an institution with lifetime longevity', higher education needs to locate itself knowingly within the broader insti-tutional context of social, civic and cosmopolitan relations that will shape that narrative. (See Nixon, 2008b, 128–130.)

Towards an Ethics of 'rooted cosmopolitanism'

A tenable cosmopolitanism, in the first instance, must take seriously the value of human life, and the value of particular human lives, the lives people have made for themselves, within the communities that help lend significance to their lives. This prescription captures the challenge.

(Appiah, 2005, 213)

Cosmopolitanism, viewed as an ethical imperative, cannot shape the pro-cess of '*really existing cosmopolitanization*'. An ethical perspective can, however, highlight those aspects of that process that require an ethical response. It can focus our minds on the moral choices available to us – because, con-trary to neo-liberal orthodoxy, moral choices are not only relevant but also essential in developing a cosmopolitan outlook. One of the fairy tales told by that orthodoxy is that the subprime crisis of 2007 (which revealed its devastating global impact the following year) could not possibly have been foreseen. However, as Aglietta and Berrebi (2007) writing prior to the 2007 crisis show, the impending crash was staring everyone in the face in the form of the massive, uncontrolled US current account deficit which turned out to be one of the most important factors leading to the crisis. (See also: Bergsten, 2009; Cohan, 2009; Giles, 2008; Gray, 2002; McDonald, 2009). Writing with the advantage of hindsight, Madrick (2009, 54) reinforces this point: 'practically everyone now agrees that the steep recession of the last two years was caused, at least in part, by lack of government oversight of the financial industry'. Yet, because global capitalism was at the time assumed to be on an invincible and inexorable 'roller', ethical considerations were deemed to be an irrelevance. There were no moral choices to be made.

That economic determinism was itself a major part of the problem. If, with Aglietta and Berrebi, one rejects the notion of the economy as a self-determining and encapsulated sphere of activity and instead pays attention to how institutional, social and political structures (or 'regimes') mediate market forces, then ethical, cultural and political considerations are of paramount importance. This adds a further dimension to the ethics of cosmopolitanism: beyond an ethics of inter-personal recognition and mutuality and of civic hospitality and engagement towards an ethics of trans-local and trans-national interconnectivity. That is not to say that the latter supersedes the ethics of recognition and hospitality introduced in the previous two chapters. On the contrary, it complements them, builds upon them and extends their scope and reach. It does not abandon inter-personal relationality or our civic attachments to locality and nation, but locates these within a worldwide web of trans-local and trans-national relations. It radically changes what Berger (2007, 114) terms our 'territory of experience'. From this cosmopolitan outlook, the local is implicit in the global and the global in the local.

That is why Appiah's (2005, 213) notion of 'rooted cosmopolitanism' is so apt: 'a cosmopolitanism with prospects must reconcile a kind of universalism with the legitimacy of at least some forms of partiality' (p. 223). A cosmopolitan outlook does not necessitate or even encourage an uprooting of affiliation and association from the partial to the universal, although it does necessarily involve shifts of perspective. 'Rooted cosmopolitanism' may be grounded in the particularities of local loyalty and community while branching out into the civic and flourishing within the broader interconnectivities of the global. There is a need for higher education practices that develop the cosmopolitan dispositions necessary for this rooting and flourishing: this recognition of the interdependency of the local and the global; this sense of the global-in-the-local and the local-in-the-global.

Traditionally, the public good has been defined in terms of what was good for the locality and the nation. The idea of community education encapsulates this sense of education as being a common good to be shared as an entitlement by all members of the community. Within the higher education sector of the UK, the older 'civic' universities and the post-Robbins, post-1992 and more recent universities continue to draw a significant proportion of their undergraduate student population from within the broad region. They very often developed from earlier institutions that were rooted in local trades and industries with which they may retain historic partnerships that are reflected in their particular specialism and areas of academic excellence. Similarly, the community colleges and state universities within the USA system reflect and respond to the particular needs and priorities of the locality and state.

An ethic of 'rooted cosmopolitanism' values these institutional loyalties and affiliations, but locates them within a broader cosmopolitan vision. The rooted particularity of the institution and its history and of the students and their backgrounds is of supreme importance. However, that rooted particularity is now being shaped by a process of '*really existing cosmopolitanization*', the impact and significance of which can only be understood by really existing people who seek to relate its impact and significance to their own and others' really existing circumstances. Conceived in this way, cosmopolitanism is not some kind of ethical abstract, but involves recognition of our global interconnectivities and interdependencies and an acknowledgement of the need for collective responses to challenges that although global are experienced as local and contingent. They are experienced, that is, differentially. 'Rooted cosmopolitanism' reminds us of the deep inequalities implicit in these locally-determined, global differentials.

It reminds us, also, of what Said (2004, 80) termed 'widening circles of pertinence'. He warned against 'the leap to mobilized collective selves – without careful transition or deliberate reflection or with only unmediated assertion – that prove to be more destructive than anything they are supposedly defending'. These 'transitionless leaps' lead to 'totalities, unknowable existentially but powerfully mobilizing'; they are forceful 'exactly because they are corporate and can stand in unjustifiably for action that is supposed to be careful, measured and humane'. A 'rooted cosmopolitanism', refusing these leaps into totalizing universals, widens its 'circles of pertinence' carefully, with measured pace, and humanely.

The word 'humane' should be a privileged item in the lexicon of 'rooted cosmopolitanism', for as Said goes on to argue 'the only word to break up the leap to such corporate banditry is the word "humane", and humanists without an exfoliating, elaborating, demystifying general humaneness are, as the phrase has it, sounding brass and tinkling cymbals' (p. 81). To be 'humane' is to abandon, as 'the abiding basis for all humanistic practice', any premature recourse to 'general or even concrete statements about vast structures of power' or to 'vaguely therapeutic structures of salutary redemption': it is to be concerned with, and attentive to, 'human beings who exist in history' (p. 61). The worldliness ('secularity') implicit in cosmopolitanism does not and should not imply any lack of *locus*, of place. On the contrary, to be worldly is to be situated – as a human being who exists in history – within the world.

***

This and the previous two chapters (Chapters 2–4) have been concerned with a number of related assumptions: that human beings develop relationally through *social, civic* and *cosmopolitan* interconnectivities; that human development so conceived is a public good, because each person's development contributes to the development of others; that education is the process, more or less formalized, by which the public good of human development is nourished and sustained; and that higher education is one phase of that process and marks the transition for the students concerned from formal education into a more complex institutional pattern of learning environments. The argument unfolds, in other words, from an imaginative understanding of what it means to be human and what it means to develop as a human being in the twenty-first century. The following three chapters turn from these 'imaginaries' to the question of how they might be actualized; how they might be realized in action through the practice of higher education. The goods of higher education, it is argued, are actual, not abstract: human *capability*, human *reasoning* and human *purpose*. These are the indispensable resources of higher education and constitute its legacy for the future.

Interlude: From Imaginaries to Actualities

The words 'dream' and 'imagination' are often confused, but one of the interesting things about dreams, the proper dreams induced by sleep, is how unimaginative they are.

(Jack, 2009, 308)

If imagination is to be distinguished from 'proper dreams induced by sleep' (as Jack suggests), then it should also be distinguished from those waking dreams that Coleridge classifies as 'fancy'. Coleridge, who knew the cost of confusing the imaginative and the fanciful, records in his *Biographia Literaria* of 1817 that he had come to the conclusion some years before that 'fancy and imagination were two distinct and widely different faculties, instead of being, according to the general belief, either two names with one meaning, or at furthest the lower and higher degree of one and the same power' (Coleridge, 1965, 50). The imagination he takes to be 'the prime agent of all human perception'; fancy, on the contrary, is the passive reception of 'materials ready made from the law of association' (p. 167). Fancy, as he defines it, is more akin to the state of free association that he himself might well have linked to his own growing dependence upon laudanum (of which opium was the main ingredient). Imagination is the active power of perceiving things as they actually are.

What Coleridge understood by imagination had been gained through his long absorption in German philosophy – but, perhaps more significantly, through his formative conversations and walks with Dorothy and William Wordsworth in the north west and south west of England. The production of the 1798 *Lyrical Ballads* was perhaps the most productive period in Coleridge's poetic career (Holmes, 1998, 169–204). In the final version of the preface to this path-breaking manifesto of a poetry collection, Wordsworth expressed the wish to keep the reader 'in the company of flesh and blood' (Wordsworth and Coleridge, 2005, 295). Imagination, they were declaring, was not to be seen as an escape into fanciful speculation, but as a state of willed attentiveness to what is perceived. Wordsworth described that willed attentiveness as 'excitement' – a state of mind that directs the attentive and perceptive mind towards composition and synthesis.

Wordsworth, in Books XI and XII of his 1805 *Prelude*, takes up this theme under the title of 'imagination, how impaired and restored'. In what has become a famous passage, he recalls how as a child ('then not six years old') he had observed a pool 'that lay beneath the hills', a beacon 'on the summit', and a woman 'who bore a pitcher on her head'. The latter, he recalls, was forcing her way 'against the blowing wind'. It was an 'ordinary sight', but his recollection of its ordinariness is what 'restores' his 'impaired' imagination. His imagination recalls him to the ordinary and the commonplace: 'the company of flesh and blood'. The trajectory of his imagination is directed, through a process of recollection and of the passage of time, towards the actual. It is the attention to and perception of the commonplace that restores and sustains the imagination – the realisation, that is, that 'it was, in truth,/An ordinary sight' (Wordsworth, 1960, 214).

Thus, ironically, one of the great legacies of romanticism as a cultural force was realism. Without the earlier emphasis on the vernacular, the ordinary and the phenomenal, the 'turn' to realism would have been inconceivable. Imagination is never idle. It enables us, as Nussbaum (1995, 31) puts it, 'to acknowledge [our] own world and to choose more reflectively in it'. It brings us back to the actual and to our place within the actual. Moreover, if romanticism was the precursor of realism, it was also the meeting place of science and art. For, as Holmes (2008) demonstrates in his study of 'the age of wonder', it was 'the romantic generation' – generally regarded as intensely hostile to science – that discovered 'the beauty and terror of science'. The imaginaries of both art and science pursued a trajectory that revealed to 'the romantic generation' the possibilities inherent in the actual.

The imaginaries of the last three chapters follow a similar trajectory. They direct us to a sense of possibility that is implicit in our actual humanity: our human *capability*, our *reasoning together* as human beings, and our human *purposefulness*. That sense of possibility does not prescribe particular courses of action, but opens the door onto new possibilities. It provides a space within which actual human beings – regardless, as the formula quite rightly has it, of race, class, gender and sexual orientation – can begin to gather the resources necessary for becoming a vital part of something larger than their individual selves. The goods of higher education are people: capable and purposeful human beings with the capacity to reason together towards the common good.

Chapter 5

Human Capability

A person's 'capability' refers to the alternative combinations of functionings that are feasible for her to achieve. Capability is thus a kind of freedom: the substantive freedom to achieve alternative functioning combinations (or, less formally put, the freedom to achieve various lifestyles).

(Sen, 1999, 75)

The previous three chapters sought to salvage the idea of the public good. However, to be useful ideas must provide the promise that under propitious circumstances they could be 'realised' – that is, made 'real' by being acted upon or 'actualised'. It is to the realization of the idea of the public good as developed in the previous three chapters that we now turn. Higher education is a public good because it provides the human goods of capability, reason and purposefulness. These collective goods sustain and enhance the public good, but by means that cannot always be pre-determined and with outcomes that can be very rarely pre-specified. The point is well made by Walker (2003, 177): 'through (higher) education students should be enabled to develop their capabilities . . . But what they choose to do with these capacities, in other words how they act or function, cannot be pre-determined'. The relation between capability and freedom is, thus, crucial. Indeed, as Sen (quoted above) insists, capability is itself 'a kind of freedom' – a 'substantive freedom'.

This and the following two chapters are concerned, then, with the public goods of higher education. I am defining these as the goods that higher education contributes both to the individuals who participate in higher education and to the wider society which benefits directly or indirectly from their participation. These central chapters are concerned primarily with the teaching and service functions of higher education, although as I have argued elsewhere the practice of research and scholarship are inextricably entwined with the practice of teaching and learning in higher education – together they constitute the 'integrity of academic practice'

(Nixon, 2009a; 2008a). The goods of higher education are the aspirations and resources – the imaginaries and materials of well being – that it contributes to the common good.

So, in this and the following two chapters, the key questions are: what goods might we expect the graduates of today to carry forward into their own and other's future lives? What notion of the good life – and of the good society – is implicit in these public goods? What, in short, is the contribution of higher education to the public good? The underlying assumption is that human being, in all its diversity, resides at the heart of, and within the mind of, the public good – the public good is not an abstraction but a sense of possibility framed within a sense of reality. The resources and the imaginaries of the public good are located in the potential capabilities of human beings.

In employing capability, reason and purpose as key concepts in the development of the argument, I am not in any way denying higher education its role in the stewardship of worthwhile knowledge and the development of relevant skills. (I am, for example, in full agreement with Young, 2008, regarding the importance of the problem of knowledge in the curriculum.) However, in arguing for higher education as a public good – and in seeking to identify the specific goods of higher education so defined – it is necessary to foreground a different set of concepts and to reinstate a different mode of discourse. In order to understand higher education in this new light, we need to re-locate many of the old arguments within a broader discussion of what constitutes the good life and how the good life – for particular people, in particular places, at particular times – contributes to the good society.

The notion of the quality of life, and the broader calculus of humanistic appraisal which it provides, offers a useful starting point from which to discuss the idea of capability and its relevance for higher education. 'The claim', as Sen (1993, 37) puts it, 'is that the functionings make up a person's being': what we do is what we are, so that 'the evaluation of a person's well-being has to take the form of an assessment of these constituent elements'. The quality of a person's life has to be judged in terms of her or his own sense of personal welfare.

Quality of Life

The well-being achievement of a person can be seen as an evaluation of the 'wellness' of the person's state of being (rather than, say, the goodness of her contribution to the country, or her success in achieving her overall goals). The exercise, then, is that of assessing the constituent elements of the person's being seen from the perspective of her own personal welfare.

(Sen, 1993, 36)

One way of viewing the public goods of higher education, then, is to see them as contributing to the quality of human life. Sen argues that the quality of life depends on the 'functionings' that are feasible to achieve in the contexts within which we are located. Human capability is the freedom to choose between alternative combinations of 'functionings' and so achieve an identity, a life narrative, 'a lifestyle'. (See Nussbaum and Sen, 1993.) Higher education not only contributes greatly to our achieved 'functionings', but also provides an institutional space to exercise our freedom – our capability – to choose between alternative combinations of 'functionings'. It allows an opportunity for what Bauman (1992, 193–194) calls 'the incessant (and non-linear) *activity* of self-constitution that makes the identity of the agent'. In other words, the self-organization of the agent in terms of a stable and pre-ordained life-project 'is displaced by the *process of self-constitution*' (Original emphases). We choose what to do and what we choose to do is what we become.

From this perspective the 'functionings' achieved through higher education gain their educational *raison d'être* from the promise of human capability – the freedom to choose a way of life – that they make possible. The 'functionings' achieved through higher education are of supreme importance, but they do not in themselves define what is educational about higher education. An educated person has undoubtedly achieved a high level of fairly sophisticated 'functionings', but in order to be an educated person he or she must also have achieved the capability necessary to begin to grasp the possibilities inherent in different combinations of 'functionings'. An educated person is, by this definition, necessarily a capable person and a capable person is necessarily one who has acquired a particular combination of 'functionings'. Capability cannot, however, be reduced to the sum of its combined 'functionings'; it is what grants that particular combination its unique significance and worth within the context of a particular and whole way of life – or, as Bauman puts it, through the process of self-constitution.

Nevertheless, much of the educational literature on higher education practice focuses exclusively on 'functionings'. These, after all, constitute the 'overt' (or intended) curriculum of higher education. Evidence of student achievement in relation to specified 'functionings' provides the basis of student assessment regimes and of institutional auditing: 'functionings', in other words, 'count'. They are the pre-specified 'targets' and 'outcomes' of student learning which are assumed to provide credibility and legitimacy to teaching programmes developed, validated and implemented across the higher education sector. Capability, on the other hand, is a major component of the 'hidden' (or unintended) curriculum of higher education. It is rarely taught or formally assessed, although it is a crucial element in critical pedagogies that encourage a reflexive awareness by learners of how they themselves are situated within their own learning. It is by means of that awareness that we begin to understand the particular options that are open to us (and those that are closed to us) and the implications for ourselves and others of the specific life choices we make (and of the further choices that are thereby shut off). The capable person cannot simply be read off against a set of abstract principles, learning outcomes, or performance indicators.

An integrative approach to the enhancement of quality of life, as advanced for example by Costanza et. al. (2008), aims both to create opportunities for human needs to be met and to create conditions that increase the likelihood of people effectively taking advantage of these opportunities. In educational terms, this means providing not only the appropriate educational opportunities, but also the conditions necessary for student motivation and engagement across a broad diversity of cultural contexts. The achievement of specialist knowledge relating to particular fields of study and the skills necessary to acquire and implement that knowledge – through, for example, scoping, argumentation, analysis, communication, etc. – are of supreme importance. However, it is the motivation and engagement of the learner that renders these 'functionings' educationally significant and that transforms the learner into a capable human being: capable, that is, of choosing how to employ these 'functionings' and to what end.

Capability and Freedom

Can we survive in freedom? This may well be the most significant question before us, and I am not at all sure about the answer.

(Dahrendorf, 1994, 18)

Capability as understood from the quality of life perspective is an attempt to square up to the implications of Dahrendorf's question and to provide an affirmative response. Human beings are born with capacities, with potential. What they acquire are the functional capabilities necessary to fulfil that potential. A good society is one which provides the resources necessary for individuals to become functionally capable – to flourish. It is that functional capability which provides freedom. We are not born free. Our freedom is derived from the capabilities we acquire and the conditions necessary for their acquisition. Luck clearly has a part to play in this, but in a good society policy also plays its part in the fair distribution of capability as it relates to freedom. 'For example', as Sen (1999, 75) puts it, 'an affluent person who fasts may have the same functioning achievement in terms of eating or nourishment as a destitute person who is forced to starve, but the first person . . . *can* choose to eat well and be well nourished in a way the second cannot' (original emphasis).

The capabilities approach, as advanced by Nussbaum (2000) and Sen (1999), enables us to be more specific as to what constitutes the necessary core of relevant capabilities and as to how capability relates to function. (See, also, Nussbaum and Glover, 1995; Walker 2003; 2006; 2008.) Sen (2002) links the notion of 'capability' to that of 'freedom': the freedom to exercise agency. Freedom, as he puts it, provides 'the expansion of the "capabilities" of persons to lead the kind of lives they value – and have reason to value' (p. 18). Thus, he argues, while 'income inequality and economic equality is important' (p. 108), a broader perspective is required 'on inequality and poverty in terms of capability deprivation' (p. 109). Sen has unravelled from this premise a corpus of work focusing on economic development within relatively disadvantaged localities. His argument, however, also has implications for the ways in which we might conceive of capability at the level of individual and inter-personal development. Indeed, the potential inter-connectivity between the inter-personal and the systemic is one of Sen's major themes.

Nussbaum (2000, 78–80) carries this line of argument forward in her elaboration of what she terms 'functional capabilities'. Among these 'capabilities', which Nussbaum sees as essential to human well being, she privileges what she terms 'affiliation' and 'practical reasoning'. These two themes are developed further in Chapter 6. At this point, however, it is important to introduce them within the context of a more general overview of 'the capability approach' as developed by Nussbaum. 'Affiliation' and 'practical reasoning' are, she argues, fundamental to our functioning as human beings: 'to plan in one's own life without being able to do so in complex forms of discourse, concerns, and reciprocity with other human beings is . . . to behave in an incompletely human way.'

Citing work as an example, she goes on to argue that 'work, to be a truly human mode of functioning, must involve the availability of both practical reason and affiliation. It must involve being able to behave as a thinking being, not just a cog in a machine; and it must be capable of being done with and toward others in a way that involves mutual recognition of humanity' (p. 82).

To make of work something other than alienated labour requires, then, what Nussbaum terms the capabilities of 'practical reason' and 'affiliation'. Nussbaum defines 'practical reason' as 'being able to form a conception of the good and to engage in critical reflection about the planning of one's own life' (p. 79). Work requires of the worker both a conception of the good and the capacity to apply that conception, through practical reasoning, to particular ends and purposes. So, for example, if I am a medical practitioner, I seek through practical reason to align my practice to the ends and purposes of healing; if I am a lawyer, I seek to align it to those of justice; if I am a teacher, to those of learning. Professional practice, insists Nussbaum, requires a sense of moral purposefulness on behalf of the practitioner. Practical reason is the means whereby the practitioner meets this moral requirement; the means, that is, whereby practice becomes morally purposeful and purposes are imbued with practical import.

In defining 'affiliation' Nussbaum draws a distinction between, on the one hand, being 'able to imagine the situation of another and to have compassion for that situation; to have the capability for justice and friendship', and, on the other hand, of 'being able to be treated as a dignified being whose worth is equal to that of others; . . . being able to work as a human being, exercising practical reason and entering into meaningful relationships of mutual recognition with other workers' (pp. 79–80). What emerges from this distinction is the importance of reciprocity: the way in which 'the capability for justice and friendship' is crucially dependent upon 'being able to be treated as a dignified human being whose worth is equal to that of others'. My capability for justice and friendship towards others is, in other words, dependent upon the capability of others for justice and friendship towards me. The capability of 'affiliation', like that of 'practical reason', is fundamental because without it there is no way of ensuring that our other capabilities can become functional.

The distinction between capability and function is central to both Nussbaum's and Sen's argument. Thus, for example, Sen (1995, 266) argues that 'functioning is an achievement, whereas a capability is the ability to achieve. Functionings are, in a sense, more directly related to living conditions, since they are different aspects of living conditions. Capabilities, in contrast, are notions of freedom, in the positive sense: what real opportunities you have regarding the life you may lead'. In similar vein, Nussbaum (2000) claims that 'functionings, not simply capabilities, are what render life fully human, in the sense that if there were no functionings of any kind in a life, we could hardly applaud it, no matter what opportunities it contained' (p. 87).

Nevertheless, Nussbaum goes on to argue, citizens must be left to determine what they make of the capabilities that are granted them. Echoing Sen (1999, 75), quoted above, Nusbaum (2000, 87) writes: 'the person with plenty of food may always choose to fast, but there is a great difference between fasting and starving' (p. 87). Capabilities are 'opportunities for functioning' (p. 88), but do not predetermine that functioning. Indeed, the predetermination of function runs the risk of denying the capability of which it purports to be an expression: 'play is not play if it is enforced, love is not love if it is commanded' (p. 88). Playing, loving – and, indeed, learning – rely unconditionally upon the freedom of those who choose to play, love and learn.

Becoming Capable

The wind got up in the night and took our plans away.
(Chinese proverb quoted in Berger, 2007, 37)

O'Hagan's (2008, 330–365) essay entitled 'Brothers' might well have carried the epithet: 'the unity of a virtue in someone's life is intelligible only as a characteristic of a unitary life, a life that can be conceived and evaluated as a whole' (MacIntyre, 1985, 205). It tells the story of two men – one serving in the British army and the other in the US Marines as a fighter pilot – recently killed in military action in or over southern Iraq. 'Anthony Wakefield and John Spahr were as different as land and air' (p. 364), O'Hagan tells us, while reminding his readers that they were also 'at whatever remove, brothers in arms' (p. 359). Both men were judged to have been highly capable, not only in the skill and expertise of the way in which they fulfilled their various and often extremely dangerous functions, but also in their unreserved commitment to the way of life they had chosen. Both provide object lessons in the complicated process of becoming capable. However, the case of Lieutenant Colonel John Spahr highlights some particular points that are worth dwelling on – and to which the Chinese proverb quoted above is, as we shall see, particularly relevant.

John Spahr was born in 1963 in New Jersey. He died in 2005 . 'Early on', O'Hagan tells us, 'it became obvious that John was gifted at sports. He was peaceful but determined . . . For John's father the great hope was that his son might become an athlete' (p. 341). Some of his siblings, O'Hagan reports, now feel that the pressure to succeed was almost too much: 'Ronnie [John's Father] would get up with John at five in the morning and drive him down to the boathouse, just to see him row. It was Ronnie's dream that his eldest son prove his specialness that way, perhaps exceeding hopes he once had for himself' (p. 341). The immediate outcomes of this intense paternal focus on John's sporting prowess seemed beneficial. According to John's mother, as quoted by O'Hagan, 'Ronnie was passionate about sports . . . And it wasn't a burden for him. He wanted to be a good guy . . . From a young age John was focused' (p. 342).

John was a huge success at school and on the strength of his sporting achievements gained a highly coveted football scholarship to the University of Delaware. 'At Delaware', his sister Tracy reports, 'he did a lot of growing up' (p. 354). O'Hagan sums up John's experience at Delaware succinctly: 'he came to university trailing high expectations, and he lost his football scholarship, which people say was just part of the bigger job of getting to know himself' (pp. 354–355). The 'bigger job', according to Tracy, took its toll: 'I think he was quite shaken up by not quite knowing what to do'. What had seemed like a privileged rite of passage into the world of professional football began to feel like a disappointing dead-end: disappointing to himself, his peers, his school, his university and his father. John had lost his self-identity and his public persona – both constructed with pains-taking care – as a highly promising scholarship boy with a successful and secure coaching career in prospect. The wind had, indeed, taken his plans away.

Then he decided what he wanted to do with his life: not coach football in the Naval Academy as his father had hoped, but become a jet pilot. He joined the Marines, entered a five-year programme to become a pilot, and eventually became a highly respected flight instructor in an elite training school for fighter pilots. A fellow instructor told O'Hagan: 'a number of his commanding officers said he was the best officer that has ever served under them . . . and a number of his own staff said he was the best officer they'd ever served under. He always had a special faith in the underdog' (p. 356). At the time of his death on 2 May 2005 Lieutenant Colonel John Spahr had notched up 3,000 hours of flying experience (many of them in military combat), had become one of the most highly respected flight instructors in his field, and (still only in mid-career) had every expectation of rising to the upper echelons of his chosen profession.

Looking in retrospect at the full span of this life – 'a life that can be conceived and evaluated as a whole' – it is difficult not to view John Spahr's well earned achievements as a fortuitous conjuncture of capability and freedom. His ambition to forge a career in sport was thwarted not by lack of effort or even lack of talent, but because he realised while at university that he had to set about what his sister called 'the bigger job of getting to know himself'. In setting about that task he had to confront his own failure in losing his scholarship and in doing so gained the space necessary to rethink what he was good at and what he wanted to make of his life. The choice he then made as to how to combine his aptitudes and aspirations into what MacIntyre (quoted above) calls 'a unitary life' was a *free* choice: free, that is, from parental pressure and constraint and from the need to fulfil other people's expectations. His capability – as a pilot, as an instructor, as a reliable and trustworthy professional – was dependent not only on his ability to function with great skill and expertise in extreme situations, but on his choice of a particular way of life that would combine and utilize these various 'functionings'. The wind that got up in the night and took his plans away was not, after all, an ill wind.

John Spahr's life, in retrospect, is an instance of human flourishing; of aptitudes harmonizing and cohering into a whole way of life that the individual finds fulfilling and that is judged to be socially useful (in this case to his fellow citizens and allies, but not to those at the receiving end of his exemplary skills as a fighter pilot and instructor of fellow fighter pilots). It epitomizes 'the unity of a virtue in someone's life . . . a unitary life, a life that can be conceived and evaluated as a whole'. Aristotle's term for this state of human flourishing is *eudaimonia*. This is sometimes translated as 'happiness' – and, of course, there is a significant body of literature on the relevance of 'happiness' to social policy. (See Bok, 2010.) In common usage, however, 'happiness' tends to be associated with 'mood' and 'feeling'. For Aristotle *eudaimonia* was not so much a state of mind as a mode of fulfilment through practice; it was associated with the circumstances within which human beings might flourish and, in flourishing, contribute to the public good. We shall return to this notion in the final section of this chapter when we consider in more detail the institutional circumstances conducive to the enhancement of human flourishing. In the meantime we shall consider some of the pedagogical questions relating to the role of higher education in the development of capability.

Education for Capability

The case of John Spahr leaves us with many more questions than answers regarding how higher education might help sustain and develop human capability. The point is not to judge the merits and demerits of the particular choice made by John Spahr, but to recognize in that choice the possibility of him becoming the kind of capable person that he wanted to become; the kind of person, that is, that he imagines he would have wanted to have been had he been looking back on his life from the other side of the grave and been in a position to evaluate it as a whole. The problem is that, in this particular case and perhaps in many others, higher education seems to have made little positive contribution other than provide a space for 'the bigger job' of getting to know oneself. That is not the kind of thing that can be taught, yield pre-specifiable outcomes, be amenable to target setting; not the kind of thing that universities do, or want to be seen to be doing; not the kind of thing that is easily measurable. 'Another space is vitally necessary' (Berger, 2001, 214).The space that John Spahr found 'vitally necessary' is off the radar screen of what, with more than a hint of irony, Collini (2003) terms 'HiEdBiz'.

Yet that alternative space is a *pedagogic* space in that it is the space within which a great deal of non pre-specified learning takes place. Such learning remains largely 'hidden' in the 'HiEdBiz' that, as Considine (2006, 258) puts it, is 'now infused with managerial values and goals', where 'pedagogical actions are now dominated by organizational imperatives, and the life of the student is increasingly intersected by the priorities of work, finance, and future returns'. It is a context within which, 'all procedures must be "transparent" and "robust", everyone "accountable" . . . it provides all the answers' (McKibbin, 2006, 6). Yet, it renders 'the bigger job' invisible and fails to recognize, not to mention engage with, the bigger questions that were clearly at the forefront of John Spahr's attempt to engage with the task 'of getting to know himself' and that are central to the experience of higher education for a significant proportion of all students.

Learning requires of learners the willingness to situate themselves within their own learning; to understand the relevance of what they are learning to their own lives and relationships; to explore the implications for themselves and others of what they are learning. An awareness of their own situation as learners in relation to the situation of others is all important: '*situatedness* in the world', as Rizvi (2009, 264) terms it. The task of higher education is to enable students to gain this awareness and thereby acquire the capability necessary to make their own life choices and develop their own life projects. Providing opportunities for student choice is clearly a large part of that task: choice conceived, that is, as 'a commitment (*pro-hairesis . . .*) to a certain way of life (*bios*)' (Dunne, 1993, 157). The pedagogical challenge is to create a context within which those opportunities can be grasped and the choices presented can be considered and their implications explored. Becoming capable means understanding that not all choices are consumer choices and that some choices (*prohairesis*) carry with them unpredictable and life-shaping consequences.

If higher education is to take seriously the enhancement of human capability as a public good, then it must ensure that student choice, as 'a commitment . . . to a certain way of life', is fore-grounded within the student experience of learning. 'The capability perspective', as Sen (2009, 233) puts it, 'is inescapably concerned with a plurality of different features of our lives and concerns'. That involves situating the student's learning within broader interconnectivities of the *knowledge fields*, *life-worlds* and *life narratives* of the learner: the three necessary components of a 'capability approach' to learning within the context of higher education.

Knowledge field

In his seminal essay, 'Interpretation and the understanding of speech acts', Skinner (2002) claims, as a fundamental premise of his own scholastic method as an historian of ideas, 'that any act of communication will always constitute the taking up of some determinate position in relation to some pre-existing conversation or argument' (p. 115). A proposition, in other words, can only be understood in relation to the context within which it was proposed: 'we need to see it not simply as a proposition but as a move in an argument' (p. 115). The appropriate context for understanding a particular proposition may not be the context contemporaneous with the proposition itself. The problem to which the proposition is responding may, for example, have been posed in a remote period or even in a wholly different culture. 'To recover that context in any particular case,' maintains Skinner, 'we may need to engage in extremely wide-ranging as well as detailed historical research' (p. 116).

That seems straightforward enough: ideas cannot be understood in isolation; they can only be understood with reference to the 'conversation or argument' within which they were generated; the scholastic task is to identify and understand that wider context of ideas. Yet the pedagogical implications of this seemingly straightforward set of claims are far from straightforward. They suggest, for example, that topics should not be presented as if they arrived on the scene with ready-made contexts, since the identification of the appropriate context or contexts is itself one of the prime tasks of academic study. Introducing a particular poem as an instance of minor Victorian verse is, by this reckoning, to beg all the relevant critical and interpretive questions and reduce the student to the recipient of received opinion. Heisenberg (2000, 140), who was himself concerned with the relation between his own celebrated Uncertainty Principle and the linguistic contexts within which it might be understood, summed up the matter succinctly: 'whenever we proceed from the known into the unknown we may hope to understand, but we may have to learn at the same time a new meaning of the word "understanding"'.

Why is this pedagogical insight important in the enhancement and development of capability? Primarily because capable learners do not take their received learning for granted. They understand that what they are trying to understand has to be understood within its own context and on its own terms, in order that its relevance for the learner's own situation can be understood. This is not simply a matter of the technical 'transfer' or 'application' of knowledge; it involves the 'translation' – the carrying across – of insights from one realm of meaning to another. Capable learners translate, mediate and negotiate 'the known into the unknown'. It is not their acquisition of 'the known' that renders them capable, but their understanding of how to carry 'the known' forward 'into the unknown': the possibilities available, the choices flowing from those possibilities, and the resources necessary to carry through the implications of those choices.

Life-world

Capable learners also connect with their learning by relating it to their own life-worlds. Again, this precept challenges those approaches to teaching and learning that seek 'objectivity' through the erasure of the learner's commitments, value affiliations and prior judgements. Gadamer (2004), in arguing that understanding 'involves neither 'neutrality' with respect to content nor the extinction of one's self' (p. 271), quotes Husserl on this subject:

[T]he naiveté of talk about 'objectivity' which completely ignores experiencing, knowing subjectivity, subjectivity which performs real, concrete achievements, the naiveté of the scientist concerned with nature, with the world in general, who is blind to the fact that all the truths that he acquires as objective, and the objective world itself that is the substratum in his formulas is his own *life construct* that has grown within him, is, of course no longer possible, when *life* comes on the scene. (original emphasis) (Quoted in Gadamer, 2004, 241)

Life enters the scene with pressing and sometimes difficult questions. As Gadamer (1977, 11) argues in one of his later essays, 'no assertion is possible that cannot be understood as an answer to a question, and assertions can only be understood in this way'. (A dictum with which Skinner , 2002, 115, and Collingwood, 1939, 39, would seem to be in complete agreement.) We make sense of the world by interrogating it. Again, this would seem to be plain common sense. Yet, in their assignments and for the purposes of assessment, students are almost invariably asked to answer questions rather than to formulate and pose them. They learn how to justify their responses to questions, but gain little practice in justifying what they see as the salient questions to which such responses might be an answer. If understanding is centrally concerned with the identification and formulation of questions, then perhaps the routines of teaching and learning as regularly practised in higher education are in need of an overhaul.

To pose a question is to place oneself at the centre of the heuristic action. It is the point at which the learner refuses to ignore her or his own 'experiencing, knowing subjectivity, subjectivity which performs real, concrete achievements' and begins to become a capable learner: a learner, that is, who not only knows a lot, but knows how to confront and square up to that knowledge. I may, for example, have a basic knowledge of quantum theory and some understanding of how it applies to the roots of atomic science, but unless I am able to relate both the theory and its application to my own interests and concerns – my own self-questioning, my own situation in the world – I seriously limit my capability as a learner. It is not that I render myself incapable, but that my capability is restricted and thereby diminished.

Life narrative

MacIntyre (1985), in emphasizing the importance of life as narrative, writes of 'a concept of self whose unity resides in the unity of a narrative which links birth to life to death as narrative beginning to middle to end' (p. 205). In what, then, does the unity of an individual life consist? 'The answer', MacIntyre suggests is necessarily tautological: 'its unity is the unity of a narrative embodied in a single life' (p. 218). The unity is narrative in form. The purpose of life is to understand what constitutes that narrative, to comprehend that unity: 'the good life for man is the life spent in seeking for the good life for man, and the virtues necessary for the seeking are those which will enable us to understand what more and what else the good life for man is' (p. 219). Life is a quest – and 'a quest is always an education both as to the character of that which is sought and in self-knowledge' (p. 219).

Capable learners seek to relate their learning to their own life narratives. Their learning shapes the way in which they view their lives, their futures and their aspirations. Capable teachers ensure that students frame their learning within this broader perspective. To be capable is not just to achieve, but to choose from one's achievements a way of life, a prospectus, a way forward. Achievements are supremely important, but their educative value lies in the opportunities they afford for life choices and for seeing one's life as future oriented: a project, a trajectory, a lived imaginary. Education is the means by which we imagine our lives into being – the means by which we become ourselves.

Life conceived in this way – conceived, that is, as the unity of a narrative quest – is a microcosm of collective tradition: 'so when an institution – a university, say, or a farm, or a hospital – is the bearer of a tradition of practice or practices, its common life will be partly, but in a centrally important way, constituted by a continuous argument as to what a university is and ought to be or what good farming is or what good medicine is' (MacIntyre, 1985, 222). Institutions of higher education exist in order that people should understand how their achievements might contribute to the well being of a society the goodness of which relies ultimately upon lives well lived. The choice is ours and constitutes the point and purpose of the learning self: how to combine one's achievements and one's potentiality and direct them towards the public good.

A Space for Flourishing: *Eudaimonia*

The number of lives that enter our own is incalculable.

(Berger, 2005, 161)

The focus of 'the capability approach', maintains Sen (2009, 235), is 'not just on what a person actually ends up doing, but also on what she is in fact able to do, whether or not she chooses to make use of that opportunity'. Rather than 'paying attention to the actual *achievement* of functionings' this approach attends 'to the *capability* to choose between different achievements' (original emphasis). Life does not consist solely 'of what really happens . . . since our freedom and choices are parts of our actual lives'. Life, in other words, is more than the sum of its functionings; it is the choices made regarding the combination and deployment of those functionings; and, crucially, it is the freedom to make such choices which provides the opportunity for living a good life. It is through those choices – and the exercise of that freedom – that, as Berger puts it, we enter into the lives of incalculable others and they in turn enter into ours.

This sense is clearly brought out in the *The New Oxford English Dictionary* (*NOED*) (1993) definition of the noun 'capability' as 'power *of* (action, *doing*); capacity *for*' (original emphases). The adjectival usage ('capable') shades into the sense of 'having the ability, power, or fitness for some specified purpose or activity'. The crucial point implicit in these *NOED* entries is that being or becoming capable necessarily involves the acquisition of dispositions which guide our choice and use of achievements or 'functionings' and render them personally meaningful and socially purposeful. Capability – to draw on Berger's metaphor again – provides us with the power to enter into the world of others and admit their world into our own.

Returning again to the case of John Spahr we can see that his journey towards capability involved a significant and difficult expansion of his moral horizon. As a highly achieving sports student he no doubt drew on and developed his inner resources of single-minded determination, physical courage, loyalty and self discipline. However, when his achievements began to collapse around him at the University of Delaware, he had to extend these moral accomplishments to include the critical self-scrutiny and self-awareness necessary to re-order his priorities and redirect his considerable achievements to a different moral end point. Being a professional football coach (his and his father's original career choice) and being a fighter pilot (his revised career choice) may require some similar skills, aptitudes and dispositions. However they are radically different life choices involving radically different life styles.

In order to flourish – exemplify what Aristotle referred to as *eudaimonia* – John Spahr had to arrange his life into an order of capability such that his abilities and gifts were selectively focused on a developing sense of himself as a particular kind of human being. This was not an ideal to be lived up to, but a genuine quest of self-realization. Higher education, in his case, does not seem to have provided much direct support for the complex process of re-alignment and value re-orientation that seems temporarily to have left him disoriented and at a loss. Indirectly, however, higher education at least provided him with a space in which to gather his resources and re-direct his life.

An institution which defined its responsibilities solely in terms of its students achieving certain pre-specified outcomes would be able to wash its hands of such a student. After some sad shaking of academic heads, the case could be reported to the relevant scholarship committee, examinations board, or whatever, as a clear case of student failure in relation to the final outcomes that in this case were not achieved. If, however, the institution stretched its imaginative reach towards a broader spectrum of human capability it might well evaluate its own responsibilities in a different light. It might, for example, recognize that it has some responsibility for enabling students to choose for themselves between different achievements and to understand the implications of such choices for their own quality of life and for that of others.

An institution of higher education that interpreted its responsibilities in this way would also recognize that human capability is not some kind of optional extra that higher education may or may not develop in its students. Human capability is necessary, common and ordinary. It is the core business – the edifying business – that defines and shapes the ends and purposes of higher education. It enables students to gather their abilities and achievements, their gifts and talents, their failures and disappointments, and make of them lives that are worthwhile both for themselves and others. To conceive of higher education in this way is to insist upon it being a public good.

***

The development of collective capability as discussed in this chapter requires also the development of collective reasoning: the process, that is, of reasoning together about right action. This is the subject of the following chapter, which discusses collective reasoning as a mode of democratic deliberation or what Aristotle termed *phronesis*. To flourish together involves reasoning together not only about how to do things well but about what are the right things to do. Collective action based on agreement regarding what constitutes right action necessarily requires of all those involved the capacity and willingness to recognize and reconcile multiple differences. The following chapter argues that this process of reasoning together – of deliberation or *phronesis* – is central to the ends and purposes of higher education conceived as a public good.

Chapter 6

Human Reasoning

Only mutual company develops the reason and the moral sense.

(Todorov, 2002, 85)

Collectivity and reason may seem to form an unlikely juxtaposition: the former somehow suggesting a herd mentality, the latter suggesting individual enlightenment. Chapters 2–4 took issue with that false dichotomy, through an exploration of *la vie commune* – human life as irreducibly communal, social, civic and cosmopolitan. Society is not an abstraction; it is grounded in the individuality of the individual. To become independent in one's reasoning is to reason with others. The mind is, as it were, the forum within which reasoning takes place: 'the individual is made up . . . of contacts with others, and . . . since these others are multiple and occupy various positions in relation to him, he is himself condemned to infinite diversity' (Todorov, 2002, 140). The argument of this chapter is not only that we *can* reason together, but that we *must* reason together. Otherwise reason founders.

Reason relies on what Todorov (quoted above) calls 'mutual company'. The act of reasoning may, and often does, require physical isolation and even solitude, but it is nevertheless a sustained exercise in mutual 'exchange': when we reason we necessarily take into account other positions, other perspectives, other points of view – 'the exchange in which we are engaged with others can be pursued within ourselves' (Todorov, 2002, 140). There is no other way of being reasonable in a plural world, no other way of doing reason. We reason other-wise – or not at all. To define reason in this way – as a collective resource – is to claim it as a public good; and to claim it as a public good is to is to acknowledge that it is part of 'what we owe to each other': so, for example, 'when we say, in the course of some collective decision, that a person is being unreasonable, what we often mean is that he or she is refusing to take other people's interests into account' (Scanlon, 2000, 33).

Higher education is one of the prime sites within which we learn to take 'other people's interests into account'. To grasp the idea of the university as secular and as committed to humanistic study and practice is 'to understand it as democratic, open to all classes and backgrounds, and as a process of unending disclosure, discovery, self-criticism, and liberation' (Said, 2004, 21–22). Higher education so conceived is inseparable from the secular humanistic ideal of the public good. It cannot be co-opted by private, political or religious interests without being compromised. Higher education as the seat of collective reason must be passionate in its commitment to the exploration of radical disagreement as the only basis for long-term sustainable agreement. Our collective problems, the most pressing of which invariably involve radical differences, can only be resolved collectively.

Collective Problems, Collective Solutions

Since most of history's giant trees have already been cut down, a new Ark will have to be constructed out of the materials that a desperate humanity finds at hand in insurgent communities, pirate technologies, bootlegged media, rebel science and forgotten utopias.

(Davis, 2010, 30)

This observation – collective problems cannot be resolved by individuals acting in isolation; they can only be resolved collectively – would be obvious to the point of banality were it not for three points. First, almost all the problems that we now face are collective problems. They are problems that cannot be resolved by individuals working in isolation. Second, the global inter-connectivity of human life now means that working together towards collective solutions is that much more difficult and that much more crucial. Our networks of interconnectivity are no longer knowable and bounded communities, but boundless spaces the full communicative potential of which is unknowable. Third, we are as human beings in many ways ill-prepared for the pace of change that is impacting on both the collective problems we are experiencing and the collective solutions we are seeking. We are, as Davis (quoted above) puts it, going to have to gather the resources necessary – and available – to build 'a new Ark'.

As I write I am snowed-in at home with a fine view across the snow-clad Cumbrian fells. I am connected to the world via email and telephone, but transport routes to and from the house and neighbouring houses are closed on account of the adverse weather conditions. A few well meaning neighbours have struggled hard to clear their own entries and the patches of public road adjacent to their properties, but the through roads remain impassable for all motor vehicles. Cars look like little hillocks entirely covered by snow and ice. Insofar as this is a problem, it is not one that any of us can solve alone. It is a collective problem: a problem that within this small knowable community we all share.

The good news is that the nearest airports are open after temporary closure on account of the local weather conditions. The bad news is that scheduled planes are unable to take off because either the planes or the pilots or both are stranded at some other airport in some other part of the globe. Moreover, certain points of destination are suffering severe weather conditions with the result that some planes that would be able to take off are unable to land. On top of all this some would-be passengers are unable to reach their departure airports because of disruption to both road and rail in the immediate vicinity. So, this is not a problem that can be resolved collectively at the local level alone. It is indeed a collective problem, but one requiring an inter-related response at the local, regional, international and global levels.

This may be a trivial instance of points (1) and (2) above. However, the 2009 Copenhagen Climate Summit is anything but trivial. Heads of state from around the world met for two weeks to agree a collective response to a collective problem of global proportions and with dire consequences should the talks fail to reach a binding agreement. The issues under discussion were at once highly specific with regard to the impact of global warming on different regions of the world and at the same time universal in their general impact on the sustainability of life on earth now and in the future. This is a problem the collective nature of which is almost incomprehensibly complex and the collective solution to which requires an inter-related response of unimaginably super-complex proportions. Given the outcome of the Summit, it not only illustrates points (1) and (2), but also provides a graphic illustration of point (3). The delegates were on a very steep and ever steepening learning curve.

Part of any collective problem is in the head – and in the understanding. That is why the collective problem seems incomprehensible and any collective response unimaginable. We need to learn to connect, but we also need to learn to make the right connections. For example, some of the connections between a winter freeze-up in a particular locality of northern England and global warming are obvious: since the latter creates weather

extremes, my snow could be seen as a manifestation of our collective problem. Other connections, however, may be less obvious: since total green-
house emissions from homes (24% of England's total) are now equalled by
road transport emissions, my snow-bound immobility might be seen as an
unintended (and infinitesimally small) contribution to the solution. Being
stuck at home means that I am a grumpy part of the big problem; choosing
to reduce my dependence on motorized road transport just might mean
that I am a less grumpy part of what a possible solution might look like.

Collective action for the common good is supremely difficult and we
humans are, on the available evidence, not very good at it. We are not
very good, that is, at building inclusive agreements that are based on
shared understanding, that accommodate deep differences, and that
form the epistemological conditions necessary for right action. To be not
very good at doing what is necessary for the survival of our increasingly
complex, inter-connected and inter-dependent world is deeply disturbing. Any response must, of course, measure up to the super-complexity of
the problem – it must, that is, recognize the need for deep and extensive
inter-connectivities across deep and extensive lines of difference. That is
an educational task: a task that acknowledges and works with a recognition that the choice is between reasoning *together* and the failure of reason.
Reasoning alone is no longer a rational option – so, as Readings (1996, 20)
insists, 'the University becomes one site among others where *the question of
being-together is raised*' (original emphasis).

Davis's (2010) image of the Ark and his insistence 'that we must start
thinking like Noah' (p. 30) is a useful metaphor for how we might begin
to reason together and how reasoning together is a necessary condition
for the future sustainability of life. The crucial question, he suggests, is
'who will build the Ark?', and his answer to that question is that we can
only build it together through a renewed 'optimism of the imagination'
(pp. 40–46). Communities, technologies, the media, science and what he
calls our 'forgotten utopias' must be rethought and re-imagined from the
perspective of a radically different kind of rationality: a rationality that
acknowledges the social, civic and cosmopolitan grounds of human sustainability and flourishing.

Reasoning Together

*Faced with an opponent who is unconfusedly and undividedly convinced of his
position, one can indeed only hope to move him rationally by arguing from the*

ground up, digging down to the basic premises we differ on, and showing him to be wrong there.

(Taylor, 1994, 209) (original emphasis)

The acknowledgement, mediation and exploration of difference are, as Taylor suggests, central to the rational pursuit of knowledge: our rationality *is* our commitment to 'digging down to the basic premises we differ on'. Different 'kinds' of reasoning can be distinguished, however, by the ways in which – and extent to which – they accommodate difference and disagreement. Dunne's (1997, 237–274) analysis is useful in this respect, since it provides a detailed exposition of a set of distinctions and relations – as formulated and elaborated by Aristotle – between the concepts of theory, *techne* and *phronesis*. (Dunne draws on the original terminology in order to clarify these concepts and to highlight their distinctiveness.)

Aristotle, he argues, works with a threefold distinction between theoretical, productive and practical modes of knowledge. Theoretical knowledge (*episteme*), as opposed to mere opinion (*doxa*), fulfils 'a logical ideal of demonstrability: one's knowledge of something qualified as *episteme* only if one could give an account of the thing which traced it back or tracked it down, to certain principles (*archai*) or causes (*aitiai*)' (pp. 237–238). *Techne*, which might be translated as technical or technological know-how, is a form of productive knowledge (*poietike*): 'techne is not in itself a useful thing but rather a generative source (*arche*) of useful things, a habitual ability (*dunamis*) of the maker through which he can reliably produce and reproduce them'. The maker 'has an understanding of the purpose (*telos*) of the things he makes – dwelling in relation to houses, or walking comfortably, in relation to shoes'. However, 'he does not determine this end . . . but finds it already established and setting the limit (*peras*) within which his *techne* operates' (pp. 249–250).

The issue of ends and outcomes is crucial to the further distinction between *techne* (as productive knowledge or *poietike*) and *phronesis* (as practical reasoning, deliberation or *praxis*). 'Production (*poiesis*) has to do with making or fabrication; it is activity which is designed to bring about, and which terminates in, a product or outcome that is separable from it and provides it with its end or *telos*.' *Techne* is the form knowledge takes when it operates within this productive mode. *Phronesis*, on the other hand, is a mode of practical reasoning or deliberation (*praxis*) the ends and purposes of which are inseparable from the practice itself: '*praxis* . . . has to do with the conduct of one's life and affairs primarily as a citizen of the *polis*; it is activity which may leave no separately identifiable outcome behind it and whose end, therefore, is realized in the very doing of the activity itself'. The ends and purposes of *phronesis* are implicit in its practice: 'it is acquired and deployed not in the making of any product separate from oneself but rather in one's actions with one's fellows' (p. 244).

One of the forms *phronesis* or practical reasoning takes is what I am terming 'reasoning together' – one of the ways, that is, that we seek to achieve collective solutions to collective problems. Reasoning together involves reaching agreement regarding the right course of collective action in conditions where collective action is necessary but the consequences of the proposed courses of action are uncertain. The possibility of collective action, in other words, is premised on the further possibility of achieving consensus in circumstances that are characterized by uncertainty of outcome and divergence of viewpoint and values. Realizing these possibilities requires the willingness of participants to reason together and to deliberate about practical measures that lie within their power and that are not governed by prescribed rules – or, as Aristotle (1955, 119) puts it in *The Nicomachean Ethics*, 'the field of deliberation is that which happens for the most part, where the result is obscure and the right course not clearly defined'.

Reasoning together requires, then, responsible agents willing and capable of working without a rule book towards an agreed course of action the consequences and implications of which are both contentious and uncertain. It is, crucially, a communicative process whereby each participant must clarify her or his own value position and recognize the different and divergent value positions of other participants with a view to gaining agreement on the right course of action. When involved in this kind of deliberative process, argues Genelot (1994), 'the first question we must ask ourselves is "What is the raison d'être of this deliberation? What at bottom are we after here"' (p. 91). In order that these questions can be fully addressed, 'the discussion must not limit itself to the level of action but must frankly speak of intentions and values in the name of which action is to be taken. And to overcome the difficulties presented by complexity, deliberation has to refer to goals of a higher order that remain permanent in times of uncertainty, such as the ends of an institution, its values, ethics, and aspirations' (p. 97). The willingness and capability of participants to engage with questions of value that have a bearing on their own collective action is crucial to this process of reasoning together. (See also, Gutmann, 1987; Gutmann and Thompson, 1996.)

The value positions relevant to that process are primarily the value positions of those directly implicated in and responsible for the outcomes of that process. 'Deliberation', as Dillon (1994, 12) puts it, 'is to concentrate the powers and purposes of those who are implicated in the problem and solution, to identify their problem, to choose their solution, and to resolve to enact it in their circumstance. It is they who must do that, whoever they are and just as they are. Everything is subordinate to that principle.' What this principle overlooks is the need that may arise for other viewpoints to be represented and taken into account. Reasoning together certainly necessitates the involvement of responsible agents. However, part of their responsibility may be to represent the interests of minority voices and viewpoints that although under-represented are nevertheless implicated in the collective problem and in the implementation of the collective solution. (See Phillips, 1995.)

To be able to reason together in this way is a necessary public good: 'in the face of the obscure and extravagantly complicated challenges of the human future,' as Dunn (1992, vii) puts it, 'our most urgent common need at present is to learn how to act together more effectively.' It is not, however, the kind of reasoning that higher education has traditionally valued. It may have been recognized as a useful outcome of the social or extra-curricular activities associated with higher education, but the formal recognition of academic achievement tends to have focused on the theoretical and technical aspects of learning rather than on learning as a deliberative process. This is largely because the pedagogical and assessment regimes that dominate higher education focus predominantly on individual achievement and, more narrowly, on individual achievement that is defined in terms of pre-specifiable outcomes. Individual students, in other words, are assessed on the evidence of their having acquired the theoretical knowledge and/ or technical skills that are deemed to constitute the core of their particular courses of study. The practice of collective reasoning – which has no outcomes that are separable from its own practice – presents a huge challenge to testing regimes that rely heavily on pre-specified outcomes defined in terms of theoretical or productive knowledge.

Doing Deliberation

The capacity to open up a problem draws on intuitive leaps, specifically on its powers to draw unlike domains close to one another and to preserve tacit knowledge in the leap between them. Simply shifting between domains of activity stimulates fresh thinking about problems.

(Sennett, 2008, 279)

There are, nevertheless, some significant accounts of pedagogical approaches that seek to enable deliberative dialogue. Throughout the last decade, Walker has documented and commented upon some of the important work in this area. (See Walker, 2001; 2004; 2006; 2008.) Quoting from a focus group interview with a final year student reflecting on a town planning course, she notes that the pedagogical process brought to them a realization that

> quite often there are conflicts between different people's points of view and that perhaps you can't reconcile the conflicts but you can manage them and by trying to get local communities involved with the planning process you can better work out what different people's view points are and then from there try to mitigate and compensate some of the things that people will lose through the planning process by having to make concessions to other parties and create balance in the process. (Walker, 2004, 139)

Almost all the keywords in this brief comment are associated with some form of reasoning together: 'reconcile', 'mitigate', 'compensate', 'concessions', 'balance'. How do we learn to reconcile, mitigate, compensate, balance? Moreover, there are three uses of the term 'process' in relation to 'planning', but no specification of the possible outcome of the 'planning process' other than to 'create balance'. How do we learn to engage in this kind of process? These are not merely rhetorical questions. They are questions addressed by another student directly involved in this pedagogical process:

> One of the good things of working in groups is that the two people I worked with came from different viewpoints from me. The one was very conservation minded and he had what I consider some quite strange approaches to dealing with issues of conservation, like he'd look at conservation in economic terms. He'd try to put a [economic] value on the landscape. The other person, her approach was very much more concerned about social issues, but at the same time balancing social issues with conservation, and I came with the view point that it's a national park but at the same time people have to live there, you've got to allow development. (Walker, 2004, 138)

Walker (2004, 139) comments on what is happening pedagogically in this deliberative process of reasoning together: 'what they had to learn through deliberation was a considered empathy by defending positions which they found unsympathetic to their own points of view'. They learned, she argues, 'the value of "rough and tumble" compromises' rather than situations 'where nobody backed down'. 'I think the most important thing', as one undergraduate student put it, 'is not whether you win, it's developing this awareness, understanding the material and that comes through being flexible in your own opinion' (quoted in Warhurst, 2001, 96).

This process also involves what Sennett (2008, 279), as quoted above, refers to as 'intuitive leaps' and 'tacit knowledge'. It is a process that is at once conceptual and relational, since 'simply shifting between domains of activity stimulates fresh thinking about problems. "Open up" is intimately linked with "open to", in the sense of being open to doing things differently, to shifting from one sphere of habit to another'. Deliberative modes of reasoning challenge both our habitual ways of being and our habitual ways of thinking. Yet the capacity to 'open up' and be 'open to' is elemental. Indeed, argues Sennett, 'so elemental is this ability that its importance is often slighted'.

The link between relationality and rationality is central to the notion of deliberation. Reasoning together assumes and requires relationality: being 'open to' new ideas through a process of 'opening up' to different viewpoints, opinions and arguments – with both the living and the dead and those within various degrees of real and virtual proximity. The educative task is to bring together the relationality and the rationality into forms of democratic enquiry that make pedagogical sense and that enable students to flourish as sentient human beings with a caring regard for the world. Deliberation is integral to collective action: a kind of 'doing'.

Education for Deliberation

Democracy is in peril not only when there is insufficient consensus and allegiance to the values it embodies, but also when its agonistic dynamic is hindered by an apparent excess of consensus, which usually masks a disquieting apathy.

(*Mouffe, 1993, 6*)

In the previous chapter the idea of *situatedness* was used as the organizing concept for thinking about some of the educational implications of human capability: the situation of the learner within the knowledge field, the life world and her or his own life narrative. This chapter uses the idea of *relationality* to explore some of the educational implications of the deliberative process of reasoning together. I use this abstract (and admittedly fairly clumsy term) in order to acknowledge the variety of relations and relationships that are relevant to the discussion. If (as I argue) deliberation is directed towards collective action based on mutual recognition and understanding, then an organizing concept with the breadth and indeed fuzziness of 'relationality' would seem to be in order. The concept does, after all, have to encompass relations and relationships operating at, and between, the levels of *social, civic* and *cosmopolitan* engagement as discussed in Chapters 2–4.

There is a moral dimension to this emphasis on relationality as the educational bedrock of deliberative reasoning. (See Nixon, 2009b; 2008b.) Nussbaum (1986) argues that, for two reasons, the moral structure of human experience should be seen as 'fragile': first, because the good human life is dependent upon things that human beings do not control (the problem of contingency); second, because the goods we value are necessarily in conflict (the problem of non-commensurability). It follows from these two assumptions regarding 'the fragility of goodness' that the good life cannot be a matter of moral calculation between non-commensurable goods, since (given their non-commensurability) there can be no standard for comparing them and therefore no basis for moral calculation. Goodness lies in our refusal to revise our commitments to people and ideals that are in conflict, in spite of the need to choose between them for the purposes of collective action: 'if we were such that we could in a crisis dissociate ourselves from one commitment because it clashed with another, we would be less good. Goodness, itself, then, insists that there should be no further or more revisionary solving' (p. 50).

This is an extremely difficult and seemingly paradoxical position to adopt in relation to others within the context of reasoning together regarding right action. Such reasoning, as Mouffe (1993, 6) quoted above points out, is in peril both from 'insufficient consensus' and from 'an apparent excess of consensus'. It relies less on what are sometimes referred to as 'negotiating skills', than on particular qualities and dispositions. The idea of 'scoring points' misses the point entirely – as does the idea of 'winning the argument'. The elusive 'goal', to add to the metaphorical mix, is that of harmony: neither cohesion nor consensus, but the achievement of a kind of confluence. Against a prevailing ideology of moral calculation, Nussbaum poses a deliberative style of thinking around moral dilemmas; against an emphasis on intellectual detachment as the defining characteristic of moral reasoning, she poses an emotional engagement with complex, non-commensurable commitments; and against the requirements of consensus, she poses the need for mutual understanding based on the recognition of difference. The moral and intellectual project, she argues, is to make ourselves people 'on whom nothing is lost' (Nussbaum, 1990, 148). The goodness is in the responsiveness of vision, not in the calculus of choice.

If this perspective were to influence the practice of higher education, then there would have to be a much greater emphasis on the development of *responsive understanding* as opposed to either passive reception or premature critique. In order to reason together we need to engage with one another's reasons. That is what reasoning together means. Moreover, we need to exercise responsive understanding within our *worlds of difference* and in relation to *different worlds* – the differences that characterize and inform our knowable world and those that define other worlds as unknowable. Such understanding is central to the deliberative process.

Responsive understanding

We might think of responsive understanding as a kind of perceptiveness or attentiveness. Both attentiveness and perceptiveness suggest a refusal to foreclose on conflicting values and an acceptance of moral complexity as a condition of the good life. Implicit in this refusal, and this acceptance, is an acknowledgement of certain features of a common humanity that remain true in spite of radical cultural, ideological and geo-political differences. For Nussbaum (1995), these common features include 'mortality', 'the body', 'pleasure and pain', 'cognitive capability', 'practical reason', 'early infant development', 'affiliation', and 'humour'. In all these areas, claims Nussbaum, 'we have a basis for further work on the human good . . . nuclei of experience around which the constructions of different societies proceed.' She adds the important proviso that 'there is no Archimedean point here, no pure access to unsullied "nature" . . . There is just human life as it is lived'. Yet she insists that 'in life as it is lived, we do find a family of experiences, clustering around certain focuses, which can provide reasonable starting points for cross-cultural reflection' (p. 265).

The point here is not to deny difference and the ways in which it shapes our identities and being, but to ground the recognition of difference in a moral project that holds good across cultural boundaries. Reasoning together, which requires a responsive openness to difference, takes as its starting point a recognition that such openness is a shared capacity and makes it possible to conceive of this world of difference as nevertheless a shared world. Of course, what we have in common – mortality, say, or early infant development – is also what divides us: your life expectancy may be higher or lower than mine depending on a number of factors, just as my child's early infant development may be more or less advanced depending on a similar set of factors. Nevertheless, the basis of any attempt to reason together is the assumption that in order to recognize and work through our differences we require a bare minimum of human commonality.

Post-Enlightenment rationality does not always serve us well in this respect. When its prime purposes and accomplishments were to distinguish and identify – to classify and categorize – the super-abundance of the phenomenal world, it was on *terra firma*. It was on less sure ground, however, regarding the re-definition and conceptualization of our common humanity. Indeed, one might see this fault line as central to the moral and philosophical perturbations occasioned in 1859 by the publication of Darwin's *On the Origin of the Species by Means of Natural Selection*: if the ceaseless struggle for life is all there is, what unites us? And if the traditional sources of ready-made answers to that question are no longer viable, where might we look for an answer? Indeed, is there an answer to be found? (See Darwin, 2009; Ruse, 2001.)

The response suggested by the argument of this book is that we begin by talking together. What we talk about may initially be less important than that we find a way of talking. That is where deliberation starts in the impulse to reach out, to argue beyond the points of difference, and to achieve mutual understanding. Sometimes the understanding may be of differences so deep that no honourable settlement is possible – in which case the only recourse is to keep open the deliberative process. This, as Said (2004, 1–30) put it, is 'humanism's sphere': 'there is always something radically incomplete, insufficient, disputable, and arguable about humanistic knowledge' (p. 12). Yet, it is precisely that lack of completion and sufficiency that ensures that the boundaries of 'humanism's sphere' are kept open: disputable and arguable.

Worlds of difference

It is, to repeat, vitally important that for the sustainability and indeed survival of future generations we learn how to reason together. We live within and across microcosms of difference: differences of race, class and gender; differences of value and identity affiliation; difference of sexual orientation and life style. Moreover, as Sen (2007) insists, we all have membership of different communities: to reduce individuals to a unitary identity is to do violence to the complexity of that identity. We carry difference around with us in our heads and in the relationships that sustain and form us. Reasoning together requires a responsive understanding of these worlds of difference that constitute the self and the relationship of self with others.

Higher education needs to work through, within the pedagogical and curriculum spaces available to it, the implications of Mouffe's (1993) claim that 'once it has been accepted that there cannot be a "we" without a "them" and that all forms of consensus are by necessity based on acts of exclusion, the issue can no longer be the creation of a fully inclusive community where antagonism, division and conflict will have disappeared' (p. 85). If, as Mouffe is here suggesting, 'we have to come to terms with the very impossibility of a full realization of democracy' (p. 85), the *educational* issue must be how we learn to live together in difference by reasoning together in conditions of 'antagonism, division and conflict'. The mantra of social inclusion is of little help at this point. What matters is the steady working through of difference and dissent on an acknowledgement of 'the limits of any rational consensus' and an acceptance 'that any consensus is based on acts of exclusion' (p. 123).

That statement regarding what matters educationally poses the educational challenge, but does not provide a pedagogical or curriculum solution. Perhaps there is no solution. But there are, at precise points – within a tutorial, a seminar group, a lecture hall even, or by networked learning – ways forward. 'This is about encouraging students to speak with their own voice and to have the courage to develop their own critical perspective', maintains Macfarlane (2007, 59). The crucial question facing institutions of higher education is how to square this emphasis on 'voice' and 'critical perspective' with the requirements of a mass higher education system. How can student 'voice' gain recognition in a lecture theatre? How can students 'develop their own critical perspective' in a crowded seminar? What does 'teaching with integrity' mean in the context of mass higher education? (See Macfarlane, 2004.)

These questions are primarily pedagogical questions relating to the practice of teaching and learning given the circumstances within which learners and teachers find themselves. In reasoning together we start from where we are, not from where we might wish to be. That is one of the precepts of deliberation. We might all wish for smaller seminar groups and fewer mass lectures, but given that even open doors have solid frames the overwhelming question persists: how are we to match a necessary sense of reality with an equally necessary sense of possibility? To acknowledge that the public good lies in the pedagogy as well as in the public purse is a necessary first step for all those involved in the practice of higher education: we cannot wait for the ideal conditions to arise before beginning to reason together about what those conditions should be.

Different worlds

It is one thing to seek to comprehend the differences that compose our own knowable 'worlds of difference' and another thing altogether to reach out in understanding towards 'different worlds' that are unknown and seemingly unknowable. As Said (2003, 332) argues, each age and society re-creates its 'others': 'debates today about "Frenchness" and "Englishness" in France and Britain respectively, or about Islam in countries such as Egypt and Pakistan, are part of that same interpretive process which involves the identities of different "others," whether they be outsiders and refugees, or apostates and infidels' (p. 332). In all such cases, he argues, these processes involve 'such concrete political issues as immigration laws, the legislation of personal conduct, the constitution of orthodoxy, the legitimization of violence and/or insurrection, the character and content of education, and the direction of foreign policy, which very often has to do with the designation of official enemies'. The construction of identity is thus 'bound up with the disposition of power and powerlessness in each society'. (See, also, Nixon, 2006; Rizvi and Lingard, 2006.)

If, as Said suggests, we construct our own identities in opposition to and at the expense of others, then this insight needs to be at the forefront of any attempt at reasoning together. We return here to Mouffe's (1993) crucial point that 'democracy is in peril not only when there is insufficient consensus and allegiance to the values it embodies, but also when its agonistic dynamic is hindered by an apparent excess of consensus, which usually masks a disquieting apathy' (p. 6). This does not imply the rejection of the possibility of collective action or of a rationality directed to that end, but does mean 'acknowledging the existence of the political in its complexity: the dimension of the "we", the construction of the friend's side, as well as the dimension of the "them", the constitutive aspect of antagonism' (p. 7). To reason together regarding the course right action should take in particular circumstances requires a mind-set that is open to radical difference and mistrustful of constrained closure.

Of course opinions and viewpoints carry with them a more or less heavy weight of authority. As scholars we are trained, and as teachers we encourage our students to sift the more authoritative statements, opinions, texts, etc. from the less authoritative. Different fields of study or disciplines have different procedures for judging the relative authority of a particular piece of evidence. In all cases, however, it is important to bear in mind that, as Said (2003) puts it, 'there is nothing mysterious or natural about authority' (p. 19). Authority forms, transmits and reproduces judgements and perceptions that it then dignifies as true. Any learner in any field of enquiry is at the receiving end of authoritative traditions which cannot be dismissed lightly, but which 'can, indeed must, be analyzed' (p. 20). Received authority constitutes a historically grounded consensus which requires unremitting dissent and discord if it to maintain continuing influence and relevance.

If higher education is an initiation, then it must be seen as an initiation into modes of critical enquiry that recognize the potential importance of what may appear to fall outside the framework of the authoritative. It cannot be seen as an initiation into a closed system – whether of facts, ideas, skills or competencies. Higher education is a public good insofar as it opens up such systems to public scrutiny and provides students with the opportunity to explore 'different worlds'. Reasoning together requires a cosmopolitan imagination and receptivity – a generosity and magnanimity of mind – that is a necessary condition of being human and indeed a necessary condition for the future sustainability of humankind.

A Space for Reasoning Together: *Phronesis*

> *But there is always a need to keep community before coercion, criticism before solidarity, and vigilance ahead of assent.*
>
> *(Said, 1993, 63)*

The idea of 'the public' is in both usage and conception almost always linked to notions of spatiality and place: we speak of the 'public sphere' and the 'public realm'. The word 'public' evokes an image of public parks and public libraries, public highways and public thoroughfares, public playgrounds and public gardens – all of which are 'open to the public'. Hours of admission may be limited and in some cases an admissions fee may be charged for the purposes of maintenance, but on entering what we think are public places we are making the assumption that we have right of access and of free assembly within the limits of the law. We go to these places freely and of our own accord in order to enjoy ourselves in the company of others. In doing so, we validate them as 'public places' located within an imagined 'public space' and thereby acknowledge ourselves to be members of 'the public'.

Some such places have become iconic in their historic association with acts of public self-assertion and resistance: places that symbolize the need (as Said puts it) 'to keep community before coercion, criticism before solidarity, and vigilance ahead of assent'. One thinks, for example, of St Peter's Field in Manchester, England, where on 16 August 1819 at an open air meeting in support of parliamentary reform 11 people were killed and over 400 injured in what is known as the 'Peterloo Massacre'; of US Route 80 ('Jefferson Davis Highway') where on 21 March 1965 the American Civil Rights Movement began its five-day, four-night 54-mile (87km) historic march from Selma to Montgomery; and of Tiananmen Square in Beijing, PRC, where on 4 June 1989 the military response to a democratic protest following the death of a pro-democracy and anti-corruption official, Hu Yaobang, led to the death of between 400–800 people. People chose to come to these public places and to gather there in order to uphold what they saw as their inalienable right to be members of a democratic *polity*.

Democracy cannot be taken for granted. It is necessarily fragile. Part of that fragility resides in the complex layering of its constitutive elements. The 'public sphere', argues Taylor (2007, 159–211), is one of the three central features of modern society – along with the 'economy' and the idea of 'the sovereign people'. Together these features constitute 'the modern moral order'. But this moral order is necessarily an order of potentially discordant elements: the idea of a public good, an independent economic order, and democratic self-rule by a sovereign people necessarily come into tension. The tensions inherent in the nerve system of any vibrant democracy are felt in both its ethical and political membranes. They reverberate in the mind of the citizen. That is precisely what it means to be a citizen: to be mindful of difference and of the need to hold differences in tension.

Higher education in and for a secular humanist society exists to provide the imaginative and material resources necessary for precisely this common endeavour: the capability, practical reasoning and sense of purposefulness that forms the civic mind and informs the civic imagination. Any elaboration of the public good must begin and end with the idea of a public sensibility: minds attuned to the complexities of the social, the civic and the cosmopolitan and to the conditions necessary for the sustainability of that kind of mental landscape. Such minds – and such sensibilities – are one of the indispensable public goods of higher education that constitute its legacy for the future and its *raison d'être* in the present.

***

In this and the previous chapter I have argued that the public goods of higher education are not abstractions but actual people: *capable* people with the will to *reason together* towards a common good. Higher education is the space within which people become capable together and learn to reason together. In doing so, they become purposeful: people with a *purpose*. It is to the theme of human purposefulness that we turn in the following chapter. Notwithstanding our divergent ends and purposes, we all share the need for direction and purpose in our lives. Purposefulness is therefore a shared resource: a common good. By becoming purposeful, we achieve agency; and in achieving agency, we gain the power to act; and through our actions, we position ourselves in relation to others.

Chapter 7

Human Purpose

*How can the longing for self-determination be brought into harmony with the
equally important longing for shared community? How can one simultaneously be
individualistic and merge with the group? How might the variety of voices which
vie within each of us in a confusing world be combined into a political statement
and action pointing beyond the present day?*

(*Beck and Beck-Gernsheim, 2002, 158*)

Higher education in the twenty-first century must learn to respond to
what Beck and Beck-Gernsheim (2002, 156–171) call 'freedom's children'.
The children of freedom, they argue, 'practice a seeking, experimenting
morality that ties together things that seem mutually exclusive: egoism and
altruism, self-realization and active compassion, self-realization as active
compassion' (p. 159). Higher education must learn to respond, then, to a
world of increasing 'individualization' and global inter-connectivity. 'While
in the old values system', they argue, 'the ego always had to be subordi-
nated to patterns of the collective (also always designed by individuals),
these new orientations towards the "we" create something like a *co-operative
or altruistic individualism*' (original emphasis) (p. 162). Democracy has
become internalized, and in becoming internalized it has become individualized. What the solid structures of collective solidarities once provided is
now achieved through the fluid processes of inter-subjectivity: 'thinking of
oneself and living for others at the same time, once considered a contradiction in terms, is revealed as an internal, substantive connection' (p. 162).

Bauman (2003) sees this as the overwhelming question facing an increasingly 'liquid' – fluid, permeable, shifting – society. 'Humans of all ages and
cultures', he writes, 'are confronted with the solution of one and the same
question: the question of how to overcome separateness, how to achieve
union, how to transcend one's own individual life and find at-onement'
(p. 17). The idea of purpose is both part of the problem and part of the

solution. How does my purpose relate to yours? How might we learn to harmonize radically different purposes? How can different purposes be combined in such a way that their distinctive purposefulness is not compromised? Purposes both separate us and recall us to the need 'to overcome separateness, how to achieve union' – how to find 'at-onement'. How, in identifying our own particular chosen and purposeful pathways, can we relate to other divergent purposes and choices?

In this chapter I argue that human purposefulness is one of the necessary goods of higher education. Implicit in this argument are three related assumptions. First, purposefulness is more than a matter of individual self-fulfilment. Purposes are defined not only in relation to one's self, but in relation to others. In order to act purposefully agents must act with circumspection and with reflexivity. They must locate their own purposeful actions within the broad field of human action. Purposes require circumspection and reflexivity precisely because they are socially defined. That is why our purposes are clarified and modified in their working out and why they are so often altered in fulfilment – because they run up against other purposes and other interests.

Second, purposefulness is best defined not in terms of expected outcomes, but in and through purposeful action. It presupposes a sense of direction, but not a precise destination. In becoming purposeful agents we are committed to particular courses of action and need to have a strong sense of what is involved in pursuing these particular courses. My purpose, for example may be to create and care for my garden. I may not know exactly what my garden will look like or smell like every season of the year in ten year's time, although I will probably know whether it will be a vegetable garden, herb garden, shrubbery, wild flower garden, rose garden, etc. However, I do have to know what is involved in creating and caring for this proposed garden: assessing and preparing soil, digging, raking and hoeing, levelling and landscaping, watering and feeding, etc. My purposefulness is manifest in these practices, without which my proposed garden will remain a wilderness.

Third, purposes are fulfilled through a commitment to action and action is necessarily undertaken in and through time. Some actions may be swift and almost instantaneous; others may be extremely time-consuming. All actions connect with other actions – an instantaneous act may require many preparatory acts in order to ensure its effective execution, while a prolonged act may be a composite of myriad constitutive acts that contribute to its effective enactment. All actions, moreover, relate to future consequences with varying degrees of uncertainty. Purposes are not extrinsic to these processes of activity and practice, but are defined through them. We cannot judge the fulfilment of any purpose entirely and exclusively in terms of some prefigured end, since the purposeful action will necessarily involve unpredicted and unpredictable outcomes. In that sense the purpose always lies beyond the prefigured end.

Purpose, Agency and Time

Homer's characters are constantly wondering what to do, coming to some conclusion, and acting . . . Moreover they seem able to regret what they have done, wish they had done something else, and much else of the same kind.

(*Williams, 1993, 22*)

Homer's characters, as perceived by Williams, seem strangely contemporary. Homer may not have a word that means, simply, 'decide', but, argues Williams, he has the notion. 'For he has the idea of wondering what to do, coming to a conclusion, and doing a particular thing because one has come to that conclusion; and that is what a decision is'. Indeed, whatever the differences between our world and Homer's, argues Williams, 'they would not at first sight seem to be differences about the idea of action itself' (p. 41). What he calls the 'centres of agency' remain much the same then as now: 'the unity of the person as thinking, acting, and bodily present; the unity of the living and the dead'. Our purposes are fulfilled through action which has necessary though largely unforeseeable consequences for the future. Our actions define our agency, but also define the limits of our agency given that we are creatures of time (bound, that is, both to 'the living and the dead'). To speak of purposefulness is to speak of agency; to speak of agency is to speak of action; and to speak of action is to speak of consequences unravelling – to fortunate or tragic effect – over time.

Williams (1993, 169) makes the further point 'that human beings can live without the idea of historical time'. Prior to the emergence of 'the idea of historical time' human beings lived in what Cassirer (1955), in the second volume of his great *The Philosophy of Symbolic Forms*, terms 'mythical time', within which causality is unrelated to the temporal as we now understand it: 'for compared with objective time, whether cosmic or historical, mythical time is indeed timeless' (p. 106). 'Primordial time' was different from our twenty-first century time, to present the idea figuratively and by means of a linguistic metaphor, because it operated according to a tense structure very different from our own: a tense structure that was animated by the continuous present: 'in its early phases the mythical consciousness retains the same indifference toward relative stages of time as characterizes certain phases of the linguistic consciousness' (p. 106). The pre-sleep babble of the infant child inhabits the realm of 'mythical thought' as a transitional step up the rungs of the Piagettian ladder.

Historical time, however, is what we seem to be stuck with (for the foreseeable future). Williams (1993) locates the invention in the West of historical time in the fifth century B.C.: at a time 'when developments such as literacy have occurred, it becomes inevitable that human beings should, in this respect, come to see the world as Thucydides saw it'. Williams locates the emergence of the idea of chronological time within an epoch that saw the beginnings of historical study as we now understand it, the birth of Western democracy as exemplified in the Athenian constitution, and the origins of tragedy as an enduring dramatic form. That is hardly surprising since an understanding of causality as rooted in chronological time necessitates a particular kind of historical understanding, a notion of collective responsibility for the consequences of actions democratically decided upon, and an art form that expresses what in human and social terms is at stake in the workings out of individual agency.

In arguing that purposefulness is one of the goods of higher education, I am arguing that higher education has responsibility for enabling students to understand that time is what we make of it. Purposes may involve – and be expressed in terms of – expectations, outcomes, achievements, life goals, etc., but they are defined and find their fulfilment in what we do: '*what I do is me: for that I came*', wrote Hopkins (1967, 90) emphasizing the ontological significance of natural, individual and characteristic activity (original emphasis). Whether we conceive of higher education as 'liberal' or 'vocational' – and, arguably far too much has been made of that highly questionable distinction – it is grounded in practice: the practices associated with theoretical understanding, technical know-how, and (as discussed in the previous chapter) deliberative reasoning. Purposes gain their meaning in and through practice.

Within a consumerist and acquisitive society great pressure is placed on young people in particular to decide what they want to be, since what they want to be can be taken to be a measure of what they might expect to acquire and consume. However, deciding on what one wants to be is not at all the same as understanding what being that sort of person involves (and, equally important, what it does not involve) in terms of daily practice. On this point Politkovskava's (2010, 8) advice may be as good as it gets (although, for following it with such integrity and journalistic distinction, Politkovskaya herself was murdered in Moscow in October 2006): 'journalists should write; politicians should make a fuss and not wallow in luxury; and officials should not steal from poor people.' All too often, however, instead of coming to a settled understanding of what we want to *do* with our lives and working our lives forward from there, we start with a preconceived idea of what we would like to *be* and then work our lives backward from that projected future.

Higher education is to a large extent formed around this back-to-front ontology: I decide I want to be a mechanical engineer; I gain the qualifications necessary to study mechanical engineering; I am overjoyed at the prospect of becoming a mechanical engineer; I then discover somewhat late in the day that I am at not really happy doing what mechanical engineers do. At that point I am in a no win situation: either my dissatisfaction intensifies (Option A) or I 'drop out' (Option B). Either way I confront failure: Failure A or Failure B. The aspirations I held, the work I completed, the truthfulness with which I faced my predicament – all count for nothing. There is no obvious *tertium aliquid*, no *deus ex machina*: no Option C readily available within the system as it exists.

The institutional inertia which drives the higher education system to place so many students in the 'failed to complete' category is a cause of particular concern on two counts. First, future generations are likely to live longer and to have a longer working life. It is crucial therefore that their life choices regarding what they want to do with their lives and how they prepare for their chosen life styles are fully worked through. Second, the experience of career change – perhaps even multiple career changes – is likely to affect an increasing number of people in the future. That being the case, questions such as 'What do I enjoy *doing*?, 'How do I like to spend my *time*?' and 'What do I want to *do* with my life?' are likely to be more significant than the question: 'What do I want to *be*?' It is not that the latter question is unimportant. On the contrary, it is supremely important. But we cannot know what we want to be, until we know what we want to do: the children of freedom 'practice a seeking, experimenting morality' (Beck and Beck-Gernsheim, 2002, 159). They become what they practise.

Becoming Purposeful

I have a single thread binding it all together.

(Confucius, *The Analects, Book XV, 3*)

Su (2010; 2011) has written on the Chinese undergraduate student experience within the UK and more specifically on how such students achieve independence in their own learning – how, that is, they gain a sense of purpose within a culture very different from the one in which they were born and brought up. One of the students whose higher education career Su (2010) has documented is a Chinese student who at the time the study was conducted was on a BA English Language course at an English university. Celine (name changed) is from a rural area in southern China. At High School in China she was fired by enthusiasm for history: 'history has been a significant passion of mine and I excelled at it in High School. It encourages a critical and analytical approach and I am always interested in the connections and dialogue between the past and the future. I really enjoyed the three years' study of history in High School.'

Yet, when Celine was faced with the decision of what higher education course to apply for she seems to have lost her bearings:

> The time when making choices of courses for the university before the Entrance Exam was really confusing for me. Before that, all I needed to do is to study hard, and follow the usual route that had been set by parents. However, at that time I decided I would not follow the route that my parents had set for me, which was to continue my study of history in the university. So I chose to study English instead. Looking back now I find what a big mistake I made then giving up something that I am interested in. But at the time I . . . just wanted to make my own decision that was different from my parents.

At university she soon 'realized English is not something I was good at'. However, she persevered during the first two years of study and managed to select a number of non-compulsory elements in Chinese history. Having failed in her second year to switch to history as her main subject (because history was over-subscribed), she decided to join the '2+2' exchange undergraduate programme (two years study in China and two years in the UK) that was offered at the university: 'for one thing, I thought it would be a very good opportunity to improve my English . . . [and] for another, I was really interested to have a look at how people from the outside world see China and how they viewed the history of China'. In spite of what she sees as her earlier 'big mistake' and the fact that she had not been allowed to switch courses, Celine refuses to give up on her passion for history.

So, she journeys outward from China to the UK to continue her studies in English, but in the barely acknowledged hope that the journey out may somehow turn out to be a circuitous route back to Chinese history. She is sailing to her goal by a side wind. In the meantime, however, there are all the uncertainties and excitements of moving as a student to a new place of learning on the other side of the world: 'in September 2007 I finally came to the UK with all kinds of dreams about the future and also a feeling of uncertainty. The first few months after I arrived were really exciting. Everything seemed so different from China. I began to live a completely different life, learning to cook by myself, making every decision by myself, and also having to think of everything by myself'. She found the reality of studying abroad challenging: 'how to do the research? How to get the information you want? How to structure your essay? And how to write academically? Such questions were always confusing me at the beginning.' She tried to make friends with students from the UK, but found that difficult given her work load and the fact that she had taken on a part-time job in a Chinese restaurant. ('Before that, I'd never worked'.)

As she moves into her final year of study (her fourth year as an undergraduate and her second year in the UK), she begins to find her feet: 'with the experience of last year, I now had a clearer idea of my study. Though it is still tough for me . . . I can handle it easier than the first year.' By now Celine is 22 and, as she puts it, 'standing on another crossroad again'. She knows what she wants to do: 'deep in my heart I still would like to study Chinese history again'. But she also knows that she needs to improve her English and that in order to do so she needs to continue her studies in the UK. So, having left China in order to study English in the UK, she is now contemplating staying in the UK to return to her first passion – namely, Chinese history. The irony of her situation does not escape her attention: 'does it look weird that a Chinese student should study Chinese history in the UK. I always wonder'.

Working this through in her thinking, she comes to the view that her circuitous route back to Chinese history may not have been in vain. There may, indeed, be a purpose beyond the end she figured. Having seen China 'as refracted through the minds and opinions of outsiders' as she puts it, she feels she is now better placed to evaluate her earlier presuppositions regarding Chinese history. Indeed, she now feels that it is essential that she pursue her historical studies outside China: 'I have greatly enjoyed and been consistently fascinated by the literature I have read on the subject of Chinese history while in the UK, most of which has been written and published outside of China and is therefore unavailable for consultation there.' At this juncture everything seems to be falling into place: 'the study of Chinese history in the UK can also help me to improve my English.

Further it may help to improve my translation skills, as I may need to read both Chinese and English texts all the time.'

Celine's story is clearly not a narrative of the uncomplicated working out of a pre-determined life-plan. Indeed, insofar as any such plan exists it emerges and clarifies almost in spite of Celine's life choices – her decision to study English rather than Chinese history, for example, and to distance herself from her own Chinese history by studying abroad. Although resulting from what in retrospect she judges to have been 'a big mistake', her undergraduate study gave her the space and time to improve her English and to gain alternative perspectives on the history of her own country. What she experienced as confusion or uncertainty – at the end of her time at High School, for example, or during her first year of study within the UK – can in retrospect be seen as necessary phases in the gradual realization of what she wanted to do with her life. What Barnett (2007) terms 'a will to learn' persisted not in spite of but because of these transitional uncertainties. Her sense of agency – of purpose – developed in and through her varied experiences of different learning environments and social contexts.

Su (2010) describes Celine's narrative as a 'learning journey' in the course of which she crossed various linguistic and cultural boundaries. These boundary crossings involved uncertainty, but also contributed to a developing sense of self-awareness and self-assurance in the learner – of motivation and purposefulness. One senses that at the end of Celine's narrative she is at yet another boundary crossing and that there will be more to come, but there is also the sense of a settlement, of a purpose having been defined and a future outlined, a sense of resolve: 'I have made the decision to study Chinese here in the UK. I know that the decision may meet some opposition. But, hopefully, I can face it and insist on my own decision to pursue what I am really interested in'. The Confucian image of a single thread which as it unravels binds life into a purposeful unity and provides it with continuity seems an apt emblem of Celine's 'learning journey'.

Purposeful Education

In the previous two chapters *situatedness* and *relationality* were used as the organizing concepts for thinking about the educational implications of human capability and human reasoning. This chapter uses the idea of *reflexivity* to explore some of the educational implications of human purposefulness. I am here using the term 'reflexivity' to denote the reciprocal relation between cause and effect, such that each affects the other: cause becomes effect and effect becomes cause in a continuing process of mutual adaptation. Actions thereby bend back on themselves and in so doing affect the agents instigating those actions. This, it should be noted, is not something that some rather special people do some of the time, but something that all of us are doing all of the time. (Indeed, the idea is embedded in our common linguistic structures in the form of reflexive pronouns that refer back to themselves – as in, for example, 'he brought it on *himself*'.) We all as individual agents recognize external 'forces', alter our positions and perceptions accordingly, and so act back upon those 'forces'. We all, that is, refer back to ourselves and in so doing gain a clearer sense of where we are and where we want to go. We become purposeful.

This capacity for reflexivity is intrinsic to education. All too often, however, what passes for education short circuits the process of reflexivity. We do not and cannot know how our actions and perceptions will bend back upon themselves or what effect their bending back will have on our understanding. A system based on the assumption that a specific pedagogical input (cause) will have a predictable learning outcome (effect) may be effective in certain contexts. Pavlov, for example, found it useful in persuading dogs to salivate. As a means of developing our human capacity for reflexivity, however, such a system is wholly dysfunctional. Higher education requires very different points of pedagogical reference if it is to enable students to become reflexive, purposeful human beings. I discuss these reference points below under the headings of *located selves*, *shifting subjects* and *discovering agency*.

Located selves

Celine's story as briefly recounted above was very much about what sociologists sometimes refer to as 'positionality': gaining a reflexive understanding of one's own position relative to other positions within a broader context. This kind of understanding allows us to think critically about our own positioning and opens up the possibility of shifting our position and thereby impacting (in often unpredictable ways) on the 'positionality' of others. Celine, in other words, gradually gained a clearer understanding of herself as at once located and at the same time mobile – located in a particular history, but mobile in her developing perceptions of that history. The fact that Chinese history is *her* history and that she is part of that history is what captures her imagination; but it is only when she begins to see that history from a different perspective and through different eyes that she realizes just how important it is to her. Indeed, it is so close to her that in order to fit it in her mental viewfinder she has to keep her intellectual and geographical distance from it. She knows that she can no longer delay studying Chinese history, but knows that in order to do so she must remain in the UK.

There is no suggestion in Celine's story that her courses of study in any way encouraged this reflexivity. However, once in the UK she had access to a wider range of viewpoints on Chinese history and clearly this both stimulated her and helped clarify her thoughts regarding her own future. Rather like a novelist she needed to clarify her own point of view before gaining a sense of how the story – in this case her own life story – should unfold. What we can take from Celine's experience is that learners are always part of their own learning: they do not simply absorb or assimilate learning as something already given and accomplished. Learning is always not-yet-finished because it requires the learner to actively engage with it, to work on it, to make of it an accomplishment. Without this personal or tacit component there can be no learning – which is why learning, even if ever so slightly, always changes the learner. To learn well one must position one-self in such a way as to be able to receive and benefit from that change.

None of this translates easily into a set of pedagogical principles, but we can tentatively extract a few pointers. First, students should be reassured that they are part of the subject they are studying – through their past experiences, their present perceptions, and their future aspirations. This is as true of the so called 'hard' sciences as of the so called 'soft' humanities: learners need to understand what they are importing into their learning and how they can use this personal import to the best advantage. This is what Gadamer (2004, 278–285) means by 'prejudices as conditions of understanding': we cannot leave our ideological baggage at the door of learning, but have to bring it in with us and then judge its usefulness. Second, students require an opportunity to be able to judge their own prejudices in relation to those of others: how do the prior experiences and perceptions I bring to bear on the subject matter relate to those that you and others bring? Third, learners need to understand that learning is like that: it does not follow a set of neat procedural prescriptions and the out-comes are necessarily indeterminate. Students should not be fed the old lie that this or that method, if rigorously and painstakingly applied, will inevitably and necessarily render up the truth of things.

Shifting subjects

A reflexive approach to learning also involves the learner in shifting the contexts of study so as to see them in a different light. By this I do not mean that a student should shift from one course of study to another, although in a rigid and inflexible system of higher education provision this may well be the only option available for students who want to make the most of their learning. Rather, whatever course is being pursued should provide opportunities for shifts in perspective and intellectual alignment. This is sometimes referred to as 'de-centring' the subject: locating the subject within frames of reference that differ from the frame within which the subject is traditionally or routinely located. Many emergent fields of study developed from precisely this kind of 'de-centring' whereby a traditional subject such as physical geography becomes re-located and to some extent redefined within the broader frame of environmental or ecological studies. The problem arises when these emergent fields themselves attain to dominance and begin to impose their own paradigms. The shifting – or 'de-centring' – is a constant process of re-formation.

This shifting of the subject is neatly illustrated by Mender (2007) in an article on 'decentering the subject of physics'. 'Researchers in all branches of science today', argues Mender, 'embrace experimental accuracy and logical consistency as benchmarks of progress in understanding the natural world' (p. 179). However, he continues, 'it is also historically true that large leaps forward at the foundations of science, especially in the interest of theoretical parsimony, have repeatedly hinged upon revelations of the human subject's place within nature' (p. 179). So, for example, 'medieval astronomy's cumbersome epicycles were eliminated by uprooting Ptolemaic astronomers from their geocentric ground'; or, to cite a further example, 'ornate Linnean description was condensed into a few Darwinian principles by expunging teleology from the evolutionary lexicon' (p. 179). Darwin, in other words, shifted the study of natural species from a grand design perspective to one of 'natural selection', just as Copernicus and Kepler formulated a comprehensive heliocentric cosmology which displaced the earth from the centre of the universe and redefined astronomy as the new 'celestial physics'. (See Banville, 2000.)

Mender sees such shifts as 'paradigmatic revolutions' that are intrinsic to the development of thought and to the way in which human beings actually think. The Darwinian and Copernican upheavals of thought 'have cleared away ossified orthodox clutter and thereby simplified the sciences by knocking the subjective center of established perspectives off balance in some productively unexpected new way, rather than by merely altering the objects under scrutiny' (p. 179). These examples, while mind-bending in their implications for the way in which we view the natural world, are instances of what all human beings do when they think. They are extraordinary instances of an ordinary process. Nussbaum (2001) argues that all human thought involves 'upheaval' because it is inextricably entangled with our emotional development from early infancy. Shifting – or 'de-centring' – is not something that a few self-styled postmodernists do in their spare time. It is what we all do when we think – and when, through our upheavals of thought, we develop as purposeful human agents.

Discovering agency

Learning changes us by changing the way in which we see the world – and our changed ways of seeing change, if ever so slightly, the world we inhabit. We make the conditions that in turn make us. That is reflexivity's defining gesture – action reaching out from, and bending back to, the agent; knowledge looping back to the knower; the voice rebounding back on itself as its own echo. That is how people grow and develop – through a process of reciprocity whereby they interact and through their interactions discover their own and others' agency.

Wesker's (1960) play, *Roots*, is about a young woman called Beatie Bryant, her working class family, and her love affair with Ronnie, a romantic intellectual from another world. It is set in rural Norfolk in England in the late 1950s. It is Saturday, the day Ronnie is to arrive. Mrs Bryant, Beatie's mother, has prepared tea and the Bryants sit around awaiting the arrival of this superior stranger. But, of course, Ronnie never arrives. Instead a letter arrives addressed to Beatie and telling her that 'it wouldn't really work'. Beatie is left alone with her loss, with her family, with her origins: 'an awful silence ensues. Everyone looks uncomfortable.' Mrs Bryant pleads with her daughter to talk to them and at last Beatie says: 'I can't mother . . . You're right, I'm like you. Stubborn, empty, wi' no tools for livin' . . . just a mass o' nothin'. Beatie is speechless.

But, then, somehow, Beatie starts to talk, at first using the terms and arguments that Ronnie gave her. But in her brave and confused anger she begins to discover her own voice. 'Suddenly Beatie stops as if listening to herself. She pauses, turns with an ecstatic smile on her face.' Then Beatie speaks: 'D'you hear that? D'you hear it? Did you listen to me? I'm talking . . . I'm not quoting no more . . . Listen to me someone'. This according to the stage direction is spoken '*as though a vision were revealed to her*' (original emphasis). Beatie continues: 'it does work, it's happening to me, I can feel it's happened, I'm beginning, on my own two feet – I'm beginning . . .' What happens in these final moments of the play is that Beatie achieves an albeit fragile sense of agency: 'the murmer of the family sitting down to eat grows as Beattie's last cry is heard. Whatever she will do they will continue to live as before. As Beatie stands alone, articulate at last – the curtain falls'. Higher education is, at best, centrally concerned with the unpredictability of these moments of turning and reaching-out: moments of learning, of agency, moments of human 'flourishing'. It is concerned, that is, with creating the institutional conditions necessary for Beatie to stand on her own two feet.

A Space for Purpose: *Telos*

Or the purpose is beyond the end you figured.

(Eliot, 1969, 192)

Purposes presuppose finalities. How we conceptualize finality will determine how we think about purpose. If, for example, we take the view that finality consists of an agent realizing a purpose outside her or himself, then that purpose becomes an end or a goal *extrinsic* to that agent. That purpose may be self-centred (for the utility and welfare of the agent) or altruistic (for the utility and welfare of other agents) – or, as some might argue, it may be altruistic by virtue of being self-centred, since my utility and welfare benefits the utility and welfare of others. This notion of purpose is frequently applied to higher education, when for example the purpose is seen as gaining a particular qualification or qualifying oneself for a particular occupation or profession. Sometimes, also, the extrinsic purpose is linked to a perceived social good and the agent is thereby motivated by a desire 'to make a difference' or 'do some good in the world'. Such purposes are hugely important and are one of the reasons why higher education exists and why (when those purposes acknowledge the utility and welfare of others) it can be seen as a public good.

There is, however, an alternative way of looking at finality – and, therefore, of thinking about purposes. If we take the view that finality consists of an agent realizing a purpose directed toward the fulfilment, or flourishing, of her or his own agency, then that purpose becomes *intrinsic* to that agent – an idea that is implicit in the notion of *telos*. Whether or not purposes so conceived tend towards the self-centred or the altruistic depends very much on the contexts within which they achieve realization. The *raison d'être* of democratic society is that self-realization is necessarily for the common good; or, to turn that on its head, in order to flourish within a democracy I must attend to the flourishing of others. (An assertion that would, of course be flatly denied by Chicago School economists!) Higher education seems to acknowledge the value of the intrinsic purposes of learning in, for example, its routine references to students 'realising their full potential', 'achieving their full capacity', etc. However, such references are invariably placed within an over-arching framework defined in terms of the extrinsic ends and purposes of learning. Self-realization, in other words, becomes that impossible thing – an external 'target' or 'outcome'.

While not denying the importance of educational purposes understood in terms of external finalities, this chapter has focused on the need to reinstate purposes as understood in expressions such as 'a sense of purpose' or 'purposefulness'. There are a number of reasons why this is a necessary focus. First, something quintessential to learning would be lost if its intrinsic purposes were no longer acknowledged and cultivated. People grow as they learn, and as they grow they contribute to the growth of society. Social cohesion is a major public concern, with weasel words such as 'broken' and 'break-up' becoming obligatory as epithets to apply at random to the good word 'society' by pundits of almost every political hue. Britain is not a 'broken' society as has been claimed and one of the main reasons it remains intact in spite of its deep structural inequalities is that the majority of its people learn together within a publically funded system of state education. Higher education can justify itself on the grounds that it contributes to economic growth, but it can and should also justify itself on the grounds that it contributes to the well-being and self-understanding of society as a whole.

Second, since learning is for life (the long haul), the only extrinsic purposes that are of value are long-term, largely unknowable, and usually beyond the end as originally figured; the immediate or short-term (quick delivery) purposes are at best provisional. This has implications both for pedagogical practices and for assessment regimes. The former, as outlined in the previous section, should provide space and time for reflexivity; the latter should focus less on outcomes and more on the process of reflexivity itself. Learners need to have an understanding of why and how they are learning as well as what they are learning. Higher education, in other words, needs to provide learners not only with specialist knowledge (which is, of course, vital), but also with an awareness of what that knowledge means to them and of how best to build on it and use it. Much of what passes for assessment in higher education is wholly inadequate to this task (if not downright dysfunctional), because it presumes to assess student achievement according to pre-specified criteria and outcomes. How students are tested is at odds with how and why students learn.

Third, our common need for self-realization and self-affirmation is what unites us; our extrinsic ends and purposes are what very often divide us. We share the need to make meaning of our lives. Were our various meanings to be expressed as extrinsic ends, however, they might sharply divide us. That, of course, is not a reason for shying away from such divisions, but it is a good reason for acknowledging that each of us is involved in discovering her or his own intrinsic purposes. Beyond our shared experience of originality (we are all born), corporeality (we all have bodies) and mortality (we all die), there is little to unite us other than this species-specific capacity for realizing ourselves as social, civic and cosmopolitan beings. Since, as Eliot points out, such purposes are beyond the ends we figured, they can only be grasped in fulfilment: an apotheosis which – as Eliot again points out – invariably alters their significance.

Human purposefulness is a public good because it contributes to a society of active citizens rather than passive subjects: people who are able to relate to one another as active citizens capable of choice and self-determination. 'The relationship as citizen', argue Ranson and Stewart (1994, 250), 'is the determining relationship in the public domain'. There can perhaps be no single collective purpose, but there can be spaces within which people come together in mutual recognition of their diverse – sometimes opposing, at times even irreconcilable – purposes. Higher education, at best, is one of those spaces, providing across its various institutional contexts – social, civic and cosmopolitan – places where agency remains a desirable possibility: an ongoing *telos*.

***

This and the previous two chapters have focused on the goods of higher education: human capability, human reason and human purpose. These goods need to be viewed in the light of the imaginaries as discussed in the earlier three chapters. Thus, human purpose provides personhood and selfhood at the level of social relations, active citizenship at the level civil society, and a sense of global responsibility at the level of cosmopolitan connectivity. Human reason and human capability as explored in the previous chapters can be similarly declined within the moral grammar of the social, civic and cosmopolitan. The schema, however, is less important than the organizing argument: we must *imagine* the public goods of higher education into new forms of *actuality*. In order to do so we must remind ourselves that the public is not an abstraction – but a *presence*. The final chapter explores the possibility of a return of the public and of the realignment of higher education with the public good.

Chapter 8

The Return of the Public

Modern societies will depend increasingly on being creative, adaptable, inventive, well-informed and flexible communities, able to respond generously to each other and to needs wherever they arise.

(Wilkinson and Pickett, 2009, 263)

The opening chapter of this book argued that over the last 30 years inequality has escalated in both the UK and the USA. The social cost of this escalating inequality is enormous. Wilkinson and Pickett (2009, 261) have shown that 'if the United States was to reduce its income inequality to something like the average of the four most equal of the rich countries (Japan, Norway, Sweden and Finland), the proportion of the population feeling that they could trust others might rise by 75 per cent . . .; rates of mental illness and obesity might similarly each be cut by almost two-thirds, teenage birth rates could be more than halved, prison populations might be reduced by 75 per cent, and people could live longer while working the equivalent of two months less per year'. Similarly, if Britain became as equal as the same four countries (Japan, Norway, Sweden and Finland),

> levels of trust might be expected to be two-thirds as high again as they are now, mental illness might be more than halved, everyone would get an additional year of life, teenage birth rates could fall to one-third of what they are now, homicide rates could fall by 75 per cent, everyone could get the equivalent of almost seven weeks extra holiday a year, and the government could be closing prisons all over the country. (p. 261)

Wilkinson and Pickett (2009, 237) offer a stark warning: 'if you fail to avoid high inequality, you will need more prisons and more police. You will have to deal with higher rates of mental illness, drug abuse and every other kind of problem'. Moreover it takes time for inequality to work its way through the system: 'inequality gradually corrodes the social fabric'. (Wilkinson and Pickett, 2010). One of the prime reasons for the chronic accumulation of these social ills, I have argued, has been the increasing differentials in income that have come to characterize the rapidly expanding private sector in the most unequal of the rich countries of the world. There is, in other words, a causal link between the erosion of the public realm through encroaching privatization and the deterioration of social well being through the gross inequalities that privatization brings with it. Although itself partially responsible for reproducing these inequalities, higher education nevertheless provides a space within which to re-affirm – and re-imagine – the public realm as a necessary condition for human flourishing and for the gathering of the goods and resources necessary for the sustainability of the public realm. If, at worst, higher education is a mechanism for reproducing and reinforcing social inequality, it becomes at best an agent of social and civic transformation.

Any serious debate about higher education must also be a debate about how we are to live together. It can never be reduced to exclusively technical considerations. That is why Aristotle chose to begin his course of lectures on ethics (*The Nicomachean Ethics*) and end his complementary course of lectures on politics (*The Politics*) with a discussion of the ends and purposes of education. Education is the cornerstone of virtue ethics and of democratic politics. Throughout the previous chapters I have argued that we need to find ways of living together that recognize our shared humanity as social and civic beings in and of the world. I have also argued that higher education has an indispensible role to play in gathering and transmitting the collective resources of human capability, human reasoning and human purposefulness. In other words, there is a public good, notwithstanding the relentless encroachment of privatization – and higher education can and should make its benign contribution to that public good, notwithstanding its partial co-option through the malign processes of commercialization, commodification, competition and classification (the four Big C's discussed in Chapter 1 above).

The final chapter sets out some concluding ideas on the relation between higher education and the public good. Idea 1: higher education must align itself with the transformative potential within society. It must define itself not as reproductive, but as transformational – not simply reworking existing conditions, but challenging and remaking them. Idea 2: in so doing it must locate itself within the ongoing democratic struggle for both liberty and equality, and thereby resist any easy trade-off between the two (liberty in exchange for inequality; equality in exchange for loss of liberty). Idea 3: the endpoint of that struggle is not utopia (literally a 'non-place', a 'never-never land'), but actual people historically located and grounded in particular circumstances; not people as an abstraction, but real individuals who flourish through the acquisition of human capability, collective reason and a sense of purpose; people, that is, who collectively constitute a republic of learning. The crucial question to which these related ideas are a response is the question of ownership: whose higher education? If we define this as the lead question, then the rest – the hard choices and the tough decisions – will follow.

Transformative Potential

This book has been centrally concerned with articulating a sense of possibility for higher education: the possibility of bringing the public back into higher education and bringing higher education back to its rightful place within the public. A sense of possibility, however, is dependent on the collective will to tap into transformative potentials. Transformation rarely comes unbidden and out of the blue. It is there, at precise points and within specific sectors, in the emergent or even pre-emergent push of ideas and practices that constitute change. Because transformation impacts on persons and practices as well as on systems and structures, it is always ordinary, gradual and local. There is nothing extraordinary, quick-fix or universal about the processes of transformation or about our relation to the transformative.

Transformation is, first and foremost, *ordinary*. It does not require exceptional circumstances or occurrences. Williams's radical 1958 credo stands the test of time:

> I wish, first, that we should recognize that education is ordinary: that it is, before everything else, the process of giving to the ordinary members of society its full common meanings, and the skills that will enable them to amend these meanings, in the light of their personal and common experience. If we start from that, we can get rid of the remaining restrictions, and make the necessary changes. (Williams, 1989, 14)

The phrases – 'ordinary members of society', 'full common meanings', 'personal and common experience' – still resonate: even in a world within which, fifty years on, 'membership' and 'commonality' are highly contested terms. Insofar as education is transformative, it is ordinary. It is grounded in the commonplace: in the common meanings and experience of ordinary people.

Transformation is also *gradual*. It happens in long-time; but, also, as Sennett (2006, 36) maintains, in 'organised time'; in the context, that is, of institutions that afford sustainability and provide 'lifetime longevity': 'all social relationships take time to develop; a life narrative in which the individual matters to others requires an institution with lifetime longevity. Certainly, driven individuals can waste their lives jockeying for position in such institutions. But most adults learn how to tame the beast of ambition; we live for more than that reason.' Sennett (1999) shows how the steadily increasing insecurity experienced by workers is making it impossible for many to achieve a sense of moral agency. Moreover, he argues, it is those very elements of the post-Fordist working environment that are deemed to be worker friendly – flexibility, team work, specialization – that are in fact creating the insecurities. They are doing so, he claims, through their re-engineering of time whereby there is an increasing reliance on, for example, worker mobility, part-time and casual contracts, and entrepreneurialism. Pahl (1995), too, has shown how anxiety is invariably attendant upon success in the workplace – although the successful very often have the option, or privilege, of living their lives in such a way that the contingent factors that engender anxiety can be managed and ameliorated through life style and life choices.

Institutions are important because they provide a framework within which continuity of civic association, of human history and memory, is sustainable. The bureaucratic drive towards constant change, innovation and supposed improvement can, and frequently does, run counter to precisely what institutions are there to provide; namely, the conditions necessary for transformation and human flourishing. Transformation is *local*: located and positioned. It happens in particular places and under particular circumstances. As Berlin (1996, 22) pointed out, it is the specificity of what actually takes place that renders events transformative: 'the situation . . . as it occurred at the particular time, in the particular place, as the result of the particular antecedents, in the framework of the particular events in which it and it alone occurred – the respects in which it differs from everything which has occurred before or is likely to occur after it'.

It is important to emphasize these points regarding the 'ordinariness', 'gradualness' and 'locatedness' of the process of transformation, since that process is often confused with innovation – or, rather, the claim that is often made for supposedly innovative interventions is that they are transformative. They rarely are, precisely because they are first and foremost 'interventions': decisive and sometimes intrusive actions aimed at determining events and/or achieving specific objectives. That is not how transformation works: transformation is deliberative and directed towards shared understanding and collective action; it acknowledges the interconnectedness of practices, structures and systems and the need for holistic change from within. Interventions may on occasion be deemed necessary, but they should not be confused with the process of transformation with which they may well be at odds.

The Democratic Struggle

The struggle for recognition can find only one satisfactory solution, and that is a regime of reciprocal recognition among equals.

(Taylor, 1994, 50)

To locate higher education within this process of transformation is to locate it within the ongoing democratic struggle for freedom *and* equality. In making that point it is important to acknowledge, however, that democracy is a highly contested term. Under the conditions of globalization and the influence of neo-liberal political values, democracy is very often interpreted as the right to accumulate material goods and the right to the unrestrained pursuit of profit. 'Never before has the devastation caused by the pursuit of profit, as defined by capitalism,' states Berger (2007, 113), 'been more extensive than it is today. Almost everybody knows this.' Viewed in this light, democracy becomes an imperial banner beneath which to assert the supremacy of freedom over the requirements of equality.

It is hardly surprising therefore that it has become increasingly characterized by the political disengagement of its own citizens. This sense of disengagement, argues Berger (2007, 36), has become ubiquitous: 'people everywhere – under very different conditions – are asking themselves – where are we?' What he terms 'the well-heeled experts' answer that question with abstractions: 'Globalization. Post-Modernism. Communications Revolution. Economic Liberalism. To the anguished question of Where are we? The experts murmur: Nowhere!' The point about democracy, however, is that it is *somewhere*. It is never just an abstraction. It requires the capabilities, practical reasoning and purposefulness of actual people in particular circumstances. Democracy can never be reduced to an abstraction.

The radical and enduring idea of democracy as what Taylor (quoted above) refers to as 'a regime of reciprocal recognition among equals' or what Honneth (1995) defines as the ongoing 'struggle for recognition'. Democracy is necessarily not-yet-finished. We conceive of it as a noun – a thing – but it is always, also, a verb: one of the big 'doing words'. It is not something that has already been accomplished and has to be defended; it is a dynamic process of transformation. Education is central to this process. It is not that certain conditions must be met before education can aspire to be democratic, but that democratic education – higher or otherwise – is itself centrally involved in the struggle to establish these conditions. Democracy is constructed in and through the everyday narratives of living and learning together. Experiencing democratic processes and practices is then critical in building collective responsibility and ensuring individual and social development. Education conceived as a transformative process helps create the democratic conditions necessary for its own sustainability.

Apple and Beane (1993, 7) offer a number of 'principles' which they see as necessary for education to become a transformative element within the struggle for democracy. They highlight the need for collective reasoning through their emphasis on 'the open flow of ideas, regardless of their popularity, that enables people to be as fully informed as possible' and on the need for a belief in the 'collective capacity of people to create possibilities for resolving problems'. They emphasize the importance of purposefulness through their emphasis on democracy as a 'set of values that we must live and that must guide our life as people' and of reflexivity through their insistence on 'the use of critical reflection and analysis to evaluate ideas, problems and policies'. Driving these principles is a concern both 'for the welfare of others and "the common good" [and . . .] for the dignity and rights of individuals and minorities.' Finally, they insist on the importance of 'the organization of social institutions to promote and extend the democratic way of life'.

The democratic struggle, in this view, is neither an educational end in itself nor an educational means of achieving the good society. It is constitutive of life lived to the full: life at full stretch lived to capacity and realizing the human capability of each individual to achieve her or his unique potential. Learning is itself a way of realizing the public good. As Wilkinson and Pickett (2009, 231–232), point out 'we have to start making it in our lives and in the institutions of our society straight away. What we need is not one big revolution but a continuous stream of small changes in a consistent direction.' The aim, they maintain, must be 'to increase people's sense of security and to reduce fear; to make everyone feel that a more equal society not only has room for them but also that it offers a more fulfilling life than is possible in a society dominated by hierarchy and inequality'. We need, in other words, a return of the public.

The Republic of Learning

We can no longer say with absolute confidence where individuality ends and the public realm begins.

(Said, 2004, 42)

The public realm, as Said implies, does not efface individuality but empowers it. The public good of higher education is people – actual people capable of contributing to the common good through their human capability, their capacity for collective reasoning, and their sense of shared purpose. That is very easy to state in such general terms. Few would disagree with the sentiments expressed and most could point to some telling phrase or other in their institutional 'mission statement' that would point to their commitment to a 'strategic vision' of 'widening participation' and 'fair access'. Institutions have learned to be good at this kind of self-justification and senior appointments are made on the tacit assumption that those who fill such posts will be adept at institutional self-interest. Most are. A senior figure in a Russell Group university that prides itself on 'fair access' recently suggested to a group of colleagues that, since his institution had fewer entrants from private schools than other institutions in the Russell Group, the phrase 'widening participation' should be read as meaning that his institution would in future be targeting private schools for potential entrants – so as to address 'the need for a re-balance'.

That senior academic lives, of course, in a different world. The fact is that, although participation in tertiary education has expanded throughout the world, there are still, as Thomas and Quinn (2007, 1) show, 'pronounced inequalities in the patterns of access by traditionally under-represented groups'. Thomas and Quinn go on to emphasize that 'participation in higher education especially is associated with privilege and enhanced life opportunities, including improved social standing, employment and earnings, civic participation, cultural engagement, health and life expectancy.' The use of the term 'under-represented' is somewhat ironic in this context, since of course these 'under-represented groups' achieve visibility only by being 'represented' as cultural or sociological phenomena. They are nothing if not 'represented'. The literature on so called 'under-representation' is vast, but is not in the main produced by those who fall into the under-represented category. What the so-called 'under-represented groups' lack is not 'representation' – but *presence*.

We are, in other words, all too aware of the absence of those groups who are relentlessly 'represented' in the research on 'under-representation': a state of affairs that we are all too aware of and that we almost unanimously decry nevertheless continues. Why is that? It results in large part because of the lingering conceptual muddle over the distinction between 'access' and 'participation'. To invoke Hattersley again (as quoted in Chapter 1), participation cannot be guaranteed by asserting an abstract principle of access for all. Participation requires not just the opportunity necessary to access higher education, but the capability necessary to grasp that opportunity. The responsibility for widening participation is not fulfilled simply by providing equality of opportunity, but by providing the conditions necessary for every section of society to avail itself of that opportunity. Equality of opportunity without the political drive towards equality of outcome is gesture politics.

Thomas and Quinn (2007, 105–106) refer to the practical application of this political drive as the 'transformative approach' to widening participation. Citing the work of Corrigan (1992), Preece (1999), Taylor (2000) and Thomas (2002), they maintain that this approach is 'concerned with creating a higher education system and an institutional culture that does not require participants to change before they can benefit from higher education' (p. 105). On the contrary, 'it perceives diversity as a positive strength' (p. 105). It is not, they insist, 'predicated on deficit models of potential entrants, and positioning students as lacking aspirations, information or academic preparation', but requires 'serious and far-reaching structural change, which is informed by under-represented groups and their families and communities' (p. 105). The development of outreach programmes and of peer support networks, together with the involvement of students in the governance of institutions, are seen as essential elements within the 'transformative approach'.

The premium placed on 'social inclusion' and 'inclusive education' seems hardly adequate to the task that is being highlighted here. It is not just that existing structures need to be more 'inclusive' of diversity and difference, but that these institutional structures need to be radically rethought in order to ensure maximum flexibility and permeability. 'The key-note', argues Scott (2004, 100–101) 'will be transgression – transgression of the once-accepted boundaries of higher education; and transgression of the traditional roles of the university. Frontiers of all kinds will become increasingly permeable.' The fixity of structure and system suggested by the dominant discourse of 'inclusion' fails to capture the velocity and volatility of new social demands for higher education: 'just as in the last half of the 20th century "university education" was superseded by "higher education" . . ., perhaps in the first half of the 21st century "higher education" will itself become a redundant category'.

Seen in this way higher education becomes an essential element within the participative and democratic culture of any vital civil society: an emergent republic of learning. (See Hall, 1995; Phillips, 1993; 1995; Raz, 1994; Taylor, 1994). It is in the context of this broader public debate that Phillips (1995) elaborates her notion of a 'politics of presence' – a politics that is concerned not only with *what* policies, preferences and ideas are being represented, but also with *who* is being represented and *by whom*. 'Many of the current arguments over democracy', she argues, 'revolve around what we might call demands for political presence: demands for the equal representation of women with men; demands for a more even-handed balance between the different ethnic groups that make up each society; demands for the political inclusion of groups that have come to see themselves as marginalized or silenced or excluded.' This, she maintains, involves a radical reframing of the problems of democratic equality whereby 'the separation between "who" and "what" is to be represented , and the subordination of the first to the second, is very much up for question'. This, in effect, denotes an 'alternative politics of presence' (p. 5).

The point is to acknowledge the importance of participation and integration in revitalizing all institutions and therefore re-invigorating civil society at large: 'when policies are worked out *for* rather than *with* a politically excluded constituency, they are unlikely to engage with all relevant concerns' (Phillips, 1995, 13). Only by acknowledging the 'presence' of those constituencies, and thereby empowering their members as citizens, can we be sure that all the interests are represented and all the relevant concerns addressed. A politics that denies 'presence' is likely to be not only partial in its view of what the relevant concerns are, but also blind to the extent of its own partiality. It is likely, in other words, to become increasingly ineffective, both in grasping what needs to be done and in doing it. A transformative approach to widening participation in higher education is transformative precisely because it recognizes that power resides in presence rather than by proxy.

Higher education gains an authority within and across civil society by ensuring a strong public presence within and across its institutional frameworks. Its prime public good is people endowed with capability, practical reasoning and a sense of purpose. Higher education, at best, is secular, humanist and critical, because within its republic of learning persons are always more important than God or gods, ideologies or creeds, castes or tribal affiliations. Higher education exists to show ordinary people how extraordinary they can be. At best it enables us to grow in humanity – to become, in Rorty's (1989) plain-speak, 'kind' to one another. The prime purpose of all education and of higher education in particular is to promote the public good of mutual recognition and mutual understanding. That is why, as Said quoted above suggests, we can no longer be sure where individuality ends and the public realm begins – because without a republic of learning we cannot flourish as learners, and without learners there can be no republic of learning within which to flourish.

Possible Futures

What there is shall go to those who are good for it.

(Brecht, 1966, 207)

If we follow the logic of Brecht's argument as stated at the close of *The Caucasian Chalk Circle*, then the claims of ownership rest not upon prior possession, but on being good at caring for the present and future well-being of the thing owned: children rightly belong to those who nurture them, carts to those who drive them well, and valleys to those who water and tend them. By the same logic higher education belongs not to those who feel that for whatever reason they have a prior claim to it, but to those who care for its future viability and sustainability and the need for it to 'yield fruit'. Higher education belongs to those who care more for its possible futures than for its past achievements. Those possible futures, however, present higher education with huge challenges – particularly so given its deeply engrained conservatism and resistance to change and the hierarchical nature of its institutions. Those challenges focus specifically on (1) the fragmentation of the sector as a whole – the need for a *public space* (2) the recourse to technical officialese as a means of professional boundary maintenance – the need for a *common idiom* and (3) the narrowing of course provision in the interests of academic specialization – the need for a *futures curriculum*.

A public space

All the evidence would suggest that public spending on higher education within the UK will be severely reduced over the next few years – probably by at least 5% overall. This is in sharp contrast with the USA where President Obama has proposed a 31% increase in education spending in order to combat unemployment and develop skills. Currently, therefore, many of the most pressing policy questions within the UK relate not to whether the axe will fall but where it will fall: Where will the cuts be made? Which institutions will be hardest hit? What will be the impact on student applications and on the student experience? Will the reduction in overall spending further fracture an already deeply stratified sector? These are questions that relate not just to management at the institutional level, but to the governance of the sector as a whole – and therein lies the problem. For what higher education currently lacks is a comprehensive and integrated system that allows for complementary and mutually supportive ways of working across the sector. Its constituent institutions lack a shared public space.

What we currently have in the UK are institutions or groups of institutions – the Russell Group, the 1994 group, Million+, etc. – acting in support of their own vested interests. Higher education, in other words, is badly placed to respond effectively to problems that cut right across the sector and require coordinated and collective action. This situation has produced a long history of well intentioned policies unravelling into the old inequalities. So, for example, the modest success in widening participation to higher education within the UK has been achieved at the expense of sector-wide planning and integrated provision across the higher education system. The re-designation in 1992 of the UK 'polytechnics' (in Scotland 'central institutions') as 'universities' only served to confirm central-government control of the sector, intensify competition across the sector, and create deep divisions in terms of levels of funding. In spite of almost all institutions of higher education now being categorized as 'universities', there is an increasing stratification of the higher education sector within and across institutions. (See Ross, 2003.)

The funding and related accountability mechanisms sharpen these institutional differentials which in turn affect the conditions of service, levels of pay and overall quality of research and teaching provision. Institutional diversification has led to stratification, which has in turn led to systemic fractures across the system, which has resulted in inequalities in levels of resource and the quality of overall provision. The point is plainly put by Insley (2010): 'a few elite universities get the lion's share of the resources, while everyone else has to put up with cut-price HE; the ex-polytechnics can go back to doing poly-type things, while the Russell Group get on with serious higher education. I fear this dog-eat-dog world will only get worse, and the casualty will be good-quality, accessible higher education'. Some

would argue that this is a desirable outcome: a return to a clearly demar-
cated tripartite system of elite research-led universities, teaching-led institutions with limited research capacity and locally based colleges serving
local needs and with largely home-based students. That would be neat and
would seem to be where, by either accident or design, the current policy
drift is tending: a top tier of excellence relying increasingly on private
funding; a middle tier of research-informed teaching-led provision relying
heavily on public funding; and a bottom tier of teaching-only institutions
for mainly home-based students. All the indications are that the tiers of
such a tri-partite system would be reflected in the levels of a differentiated
fee structure, which the elite institutions routinely argue is essential if they
are to maintain their pinnacle of excellence (or, more accurately, their
monopoly on excellence).

Any such system would legitimize existing funding discrepancies and
deepen the structural inequalities within and across the higher education
sector. A widening of the funding gap between institutions and of student
fee differentials would inevitably follow. It would amount to a disintegration of the higher education sector – a disintegration which would, particularly at a time of financial stringency, further restrict the social mobility
and the intellectual and social aspirations of the least advantaged and
thereby reinforce the social divisions and economic divides within society. Any hope of higher education becoming an open, accessible and flexible network of provision would be lost. Those with any informed sense of
the social and economic history of higher education know this to be the
case. To be a public good higher education needs to join up, link up and
share the available resources across the sector – to locate itself within what
Archer and others (2003, 201) term 'partnerships and networks of action'.
It needs to become a shared public space that is greater than the sum of its
institutional parts.

A common idiom

Trilling, the American cultural and literary critic, wrote over fifty years ago:

> [A] spectre haunts our culture – it is that people will eventually be unable
> to say, 'They fell in love and married,' . . . but will as a matter of course
> say, 'Their libidinal impulses being reciprocal, they activated their indi-
> vidual erotic drives and integrated them within the same frame of refer-
> ence.' Now this is not the language of abstract thought or of any kind of
> thought. It is the language of non-thought. (Trilling, 1951, 285)

Trilling is not here taking a tilt at precise, specialist language, or at language that in order to fulfil its function is necessarily technical. He is pointing to the tendency, as he perceived it, to express ordinary, common meanings associated with ordinary, shared experiences in a language that is neither common nor shared. Moreover, he is claiming that this tendency towards linguistic abstraction has the effect of reducing our potential as sentient human beings. It constitutes, as he puts it, 'a threat to the emotions and thus to life itself'.

Skidelsky (2009, xv) makes a similar point with regard to what he terms the 'linguistic imperialism' of economics, which 'appropriates important words in the common lexicon, like "rational", and gives them technical meanings which over time change their ordinary meanings and the understandings which they express'. This, he claims, 'amounts to a huge project to reshape humanity into people who believe the things economists believe about them' and in effect licences 'financial innovation beyond the bounds of ordinary understanding'. It is not just that language slides and slips from shared, public understandings, but that these understandings themselves become colonized and restricted.

The argument here is not against the precise use of language which allows for fine distinctions to be drawn by those for whom such distinctions are an essential tool of their trade, but against linguistic usage which changes and even distorts our shared everyday understandings. Within higher education this process has been particularly marked. To take but one example, the word 'skill' now covers so many different things that, as Inglis and Aers (2008, 170–171) point out, 'it is in danger of vacuity, that is, of having so many applications it means very little'. The notion of purposeful action is central to the meaning of 'skill': 'a skill is an accomplishment of a person directed to a purpose'. It is necessarily 'subordinate to and an aspect of the deployment of a craft, which may be thought of as a coordinated battery of techniques'. To acquire a skill is not only a matter of being able to employ that skill but also of having an understanding of the context within which one would employ it and of why one would employ it.

Indeed, the language of higher education – the language used, that is, to explain and communicate the educational processes associated with higher education – has become increasingly bureaucratic, managerial and exclusive. It collapses all human reasoning into the kind of reasoning whose 'outcomes' can be 'pre-specified' with reference to specific 'targets'. Thus, the kind of deliberative reasoning discussed in Chapter 6 is simply not recognized or is forced to present itself in the guise of technical or technological know-how. The dominant officialese of 'course management' and 'quality assurance' ensures that the epistemological premises of what I argue are the most significant forms of human reasoning are denied. Uncertainty, indeterminacy and irreducible complexity are simply unthinkable from an epistemological perspective which requires us to know what we will have learnt prior to our having learnt it.

What has been largely lost – or at least obscured – in higher education is a common idiom: an idiom and a sensibility that reflect the ordinariness of education and grounds education in the commonplace of everyday experience. To reclaim such an idiom for higher education is essential, since a common idiom of education and learning is itself one of the indispensible public goods of higher education. One of the prime purposes of higher education, in other words, is to assert and explain the value of learning in and for society. It can only fulfil this ambassadorial role if it has at its disposal a language – and a style – that enables it to connect with people's everyday experience of learning. 'British universities', as Hoggart (1982, 26) put it, 'are not wholly or simply subservient to State or government, or to local businessmen' – and the same is true now as then of not only British but also North American institutions of higher education – 'they have a lot of freedom and on the whole it is *real* freedom, freedom to say and do a great deal' (original emphasis). To use that freedom for the public good – 'to say and do a great deal' – higher education requires a public language, a common idiom.

A futures curriculum

To argue for a common idiom for higher education is not an argument against the process of specialization as such. As Collini (1993) in his introduction to C. P. Snow's *The Two Cultures* remarks, that process 'is the precondition of intellectual progress, and often represents an impressive refinement of concepts and techniques' (p. lvi). The interesting questions, Collini suggests, are about the ways in which particular specialisms 'relate to the wider culture and the impact they have upon discussion of those matters which can never be reduced, without remainder, to the preserve of one academic discipline' (p. lvi). What is required is 'the growth of the intellectual equivalent of bilingualism, a capacity not only to exercise the language of our respective specialisms, but also to attend to, learn from, and eventually contribute to wider cultural conversations' (p. lvii). Somehow, Collini seems to be suggesting, specialisms have to become neither so narrow that they rule themselves out of the 'wider cultural conversations' nor so broad that they have nothing to contribute to such conversations. Where the line is drawn is largely a matter of independent judgement, but the judgement itself is to a considerable extent culturally and historically determined.

In the fifth and most recent edition of his iconic text on the American research university, Kerr (2001, 216) claims that 'subject matter specialization increases, breaking knowledge into tinier and tinier topics'. Zemsky's (2009) wide-ranging and critical review of the debates relating to the wider system of higher education in the USA suggests breadth is less of an issue in America than in the UK, where the response to the breadth versus specialization issue is highly ambivalent. For example, 'combined' degrees (combining, that is, more than one specialism) continue to be treated with some scepticism. On the other hand, the introduction of PPE (Philosophy, Politics and Economics) at Balliol College, Oxford University, in the 1920s, to supersede 'Greats' (Philosophy and Ancient History), has proved to be one of the great interdisciplinary successes of the last century. (Interestingly, PPE was introduced because 'Greats' was no longer considered relevant for those entering the civil service. It was thus initially known as 'Modern Greats' and was seen as a response to the changing requirements of a post-Great World War society. It was in a sense Oxford's belated farewell to the Edwardian era. The impact of the course can be gauged by the fact that there are now over forty institutions of higher education across the world offering a philosophy, politics and economics taught combination.)

Nevertheless, specialization remains the shibboleth of the UK higher education curriculum particularly within the older institutions. New and emergent fields of study that draw eclectically on a range of specialist areas are particularly vulnerable and often find it necessary to nestle under the protective wing of a well established discipline. Thus, for example, environmental studies, while defining itself as a broad interdisciplinary field, tends to emphasize its links to the more established specialism such as environmental science or even politics, economics and sociology. Women's studies, which was first established in 1970 at what is now San Diego State University, although more independent and to some extent autonomous, has found it increasingly difficult to survive within the UK higher education system. Specialization is equated with 'hard' – 'hard' (as in indisputable) facts; 'hard' (as in quantifiable) data; 'hard' (as in predictive) science. Breadth, on the other hand, is suspected of being 'soft' – 'soft' (as in disputable) findings; 'soft' (as in qualitative) data; 'soft' (as in discursive) interpretation. Specialization builds on the firm foundations of what is known; breadth acknowledges the fuzzy uncertainty of the future.

A futures curriculum for higher education would require a bolder and riskier mediation between the claims of established specialist areas and those of new and emergent fields of study. It would provide students with the resources necessary to become flexible in their crossing of intellectual boundaries, open and receptive to new ideas and practices, collaborative and confident in working with others, and capable of seeing their own area of specialist expertise in a wider context. This can only be achieved by broadening the base of curriculum provision and ensuring that all students are exposed to a range of ideas and viewpoints, to different modes of thinking and understanding, and to a variety of communicative and discursive forms. Isolated initiatives, however innovative they may be, are not sufficient. Institutions will need to address the issue holistically and build a shared understanding across all members of faculty that this is the way forward into the future.

A number of institutions of higher education have already pushed forward the boundaries in this area. The University of Melbourne, for example, initiated a radical restructuring exercise in 2007 to broaden out its undergraduate curriculum through what it calls 'new generation' degrees that comprise a substantial 'breadth studies' component for all students. The 'Melbourne Model' as it has come to be known also provides alternative exit routes through to the workforce, graduate professional degrees and post-graduate research degrees. Harvard, Hong Kong and Yale have developed similar programmes. In the UK the University of Aberdeen is embarking on an ambitious programme of curriculum reform aimed at 'enhancing' student study through a range of courses that would run parallel to their main subject. These complementary courses are 'designed to consider and contrast different methods of inquiry' and examine 'real world problems' – topics include risk in society, science and the media, the health and wealth of nations and sustainability. The Aberdeen model is also committed to ensuring maximum flexibility by establishing two further exit qualifications (a certificate after one year and a diploma after two years) and flexible entry to and exit from any year of the degree programme in order to accommodate breaks in study (University of Aberdeen, 2009).

These institution-wide reforms refuse any easy dichotomy between 'depth' and 'breadth'. They acknowledge that in an increasingly interconnected world 'breadth' is itself a constituent of the 'depth' dimension. The ability to locate and relocate specialist knowledge and expertise in a variety of contexts – to be creative in its application and imaginative in its potential for transfer – will become increasingly valuable in a rapidly changing world. Similarly, the need for flexibility in course provision and in the accreditation of diverse achievements – at different levels of achievement – will be essential if higher education is to meet the needs and expectations of future generations of students. The idea that 'breadth' dilutes or compromises 'depth' of study must be challenged not just on pragmatic grounds but on epistemological grounds. A futures curriculum has at its core a notion of knowledge as infinitely inter-connective and end-lessly and unpredictably engaging. For, as Heisenberg (2000, 140) puts it, 'the existing scientific concepts cover always only a very limited part of real-ity, and the other part that has not yet been understood is infinite'.

***

How would we know that the public had returned? We would know because the public is not an abstraction, but people drawn from all walks of life and with widely differing backgrounds and aspirations – real people whose agency is defined in and through their social and civic relations and their care for the world. We would know because the people that comprise the public would bring with them the human resources of capability, reason-ing and purpose, so that through the development of these common goods they themselves might flourish and enable others to flourish. We would know because the space of learning – the republic of learning – that we call higher education would respond to the new ways of knowing and under-standing that the people brought with them. There would be a collective purpose, a common idiom and a sense of possible futures.

Coda: A Sense of Possibility

To pass freely through open doors, it is necessary to respect the fact that they have solid frames. This principle, by which the old professor had always lived, is simply a requisite of the sense of reality. But if there is a sense of reality, and no one will doubt that it has its justification for existing, then there must also be something we can call a sense of possibility.

(Musil, 1997, 10–11)

To define something or other as 'impossible' is to signal that it is beyond our capacities and capabilities: regardless of our efforts the external constraints are such that achievement is not an option. (However much I may wish to walk on my hands up a steep hillside it simply is not going to happen.) Whatever the 'something or other' may be it lies beyond the scope of our agency – our doing. If, on the other hand, we define something as 'probable' (or 'improbable'), then we signal that it may very well happen (or not happen) for good or ill regardless of our wishes and regardless of anything we may or may not do. (My wanting it not to rain today will not affect the probability of it pouring down.) Again, it lies beyond the scope of our agency – our doing. To define our 'something or other' as 'possible', however, is to recall agency, since what is deemed to be possible can only come about through our actions. (Running up a steep hillside may tax me to my physical limits, but nevertheless falls within the bounds of what is achievable.) Possibility requires agency – human action, human potency – for its realization. That, anyway, would seem to be the view of Musil's 'old professor' for whom 'a sense of possibility' is premised on 'a sense of reality'.

The global economic downturn that we are currently experiencing encourages fatalism: a lot more things now seem 'impossible' for a lot more people; a lot of things are either 'probable' or 'improbable' regardless of how good, bad or indifferent we may consider ourselves to be. We seem to live in a world where things happen to us rather than a world where we make things happen. It is a world of uncertainty where, as Heaney

(2006, 13) puts it, 'anything can happen' and 'ground gives'. As I have tried to argue throughout this book, however, that uncertainty may provide us with a stark sense of reality regarding where we find ourselves and how we finished up here; and, that sense of reality may, in turn, prompt new imaginings and a renewed sense of possibility. Higher education in the UK and elsewhere would seem to be facing a bleak future: fewer students, staff redundancies, campus closures, etc. This is in large part because within the UK politicians on all sides seem to be of the misguided view that the long term solution to global downturn is to reduce the budget deficit by cuts in public spending. It is in other words a consequence not of the slump itself, but of a particular policy response to it. The responsibility of academics in this situation is clear: to seek to understand, to respond on the basis of that shared understanding and to find alternative ways forward.

Stiglitz, in his Nobel Prize Lecture of 2001, put it like this:

We have the good fortune to live in democracies, in which individuals can fight for their perception of what a better world might be like. We as academics have the good fortune to be further protected by our academic freedom. With freedom comes responsibility: the responsibility to use that freedom to do what we can to ensure that the world of the future be one in which there is not only greater economic prosperity, but also more social justice. (Stiglitz, 2001)

If Stiglitz is right then academics and indeed all those who care for the future of higher education have some huge tasks ahead: the intellectual task of defining the ends and purposes of higher education, the imaginative task of reorienting higher education for the needs and aspirations of future generations, and the practical task of ensuring that higher education works at the systems level, the level of institutional structure, and the levels of curriculum and pedagogy. Throughout this book I have argued that these tasks require collective understanding and collective action. The great challenge facing higher education is to re-locate itself at the centre of civic society as an open and permeable space of learning within which people are able to find a place to grow and reach out.

Higher education will have to change and adapt – not as a knee-jerk reaction to misguided policies on deficit reduction through public spending cuts, but because the needs and aspirations of each generation differ from those of previous generations. The world is changing and if higher education is to comprehend how it is changing and how change impacts upon our living and learning, then it must adapt and develop new models and new ways of working. In a society as liquid and fluid as the one in which we live, higher education must have both place and space. It must be local and ubiquitous, real and virtual, 'out there' and 'in the head'. It must seek to ensure that, as far as possible, everything is connected to everything else. The public goods of higher education lie not in its economic benefits (significant and important though these may be), but in the capability, rationality and purposefulness of real people. Higher education is a public good because it enables us, as Nussbaum (1997, 10) puts it, 'to see [ourselves] not simply as citizens of some local region or group but also, and above all, as human beings bound to all other human beings by ties of recognition and concern'. Having seen ourselves in this way, it is incumbent upon us to ensure that the goods of higher education are available for future generations.

References

Aglietta, M. and Berrebi, L. (2007) *Desordres dans le Capitalisme Mondial*. Paris: Odile Jacob.

Ali, T. (2009) Death of a comrade (Peter Gowan: 1946–2009), *New Left Review* (Second Series), 59 (September/October), pp. 39–48.

Appiah, K. A. (2006) *Cosmopolitanism: Ethics in a World of Strangers*. New York: W.W. Norton.

—(2005) *The Ethics of Identity*. Princeton: Princeton University Press.

Apple, M. W. and Beane, J. A. (eds) (1999) *Democratic Schools: Lessons from the Chalkface*. Buckingham: Open University Press.

Archer, L., Hutchings, M., Leathwood, C. and Ross, A. (2003) Widening participation in higher education: implications for policy and practice, in L. Archer, M. Hutchings and A. Ross with C. Leathwood, R. Gilchrist and D. Phillips, *Higher Education and Social Class: Issues of Exclusion and Inclusion*. London and New York: RoutledgeFalmer, pp. 193–201.

Archibugi, D. (2008) *The Global Commonwealth of Citizens: Toward Cosmopolitan Democracy*. Princeton: Princeton University Press.

—(2002) Demos and Cosmopolis, *New Left Review* (Second Series), 13 (January/February), pp. 24–38.

—(2000) Cosmopolitan Democracy, *New Left Review* (Second Series), 4 (July/August), pp. 137–150.

—(1998) *The Human Condition*. Chicago: University of Chicago Press.

Arendt, H. (1998) *The Human Condition*. Chicago and London: University of Chicago Press (2nd Edition).

Aristotle (1992) *The Politics*. (Trans. T. A. Sinclair, revised J. Saunders) London: Penguin Books.

Aristotle (1955) *The Ethics of Aristotle: The Nicomachean Ethics* (Trans. J. A. K. Thompson and revised by H. Tredennick) London: Penguin Books.

Aronowitz, S. (2000) *The Knowledge Factory: Dismantling the Corporate University and Creating True Higher Learning*. Boston: Beacon Press.

Atwood, M. (2008) *Payback: Debt and the Shadow Side of Wealth*. London: Bloomsbury Publishing Plc.

Banville, J. (2000) *The Revolution Trilogy: Doctor Copernicus, Kepler, The Newton Letter*. London, Basingstoke and Oxford: Picador/Pan Macmillan Ltd.

Barnett, R. (2007) *A Will to Learn: Being a Student in an Age of Uncertainty*. Maidenhead and Philadelphia: Open University Press/McGraw-Hill Education.

—(1999) *Realizing the University in an Age of Supercomplexity*. Buckingham: SRHE/Open University Press.

Bauman, Z. (2003) *Liquid Love: On the Frailty of Human Bonds*. Cambridge: Polity.

—(1992) *Intimations of Postmodernity*. London: Routledge.

Beck, U. (2006) *The Cosmopolitan Vision*. (Trans. C. Cronin) Cambridge: Polity Press.

—(2004) Theses for an extensive reform of education, in F. Inglis (ed.) *Education and the Good Society*. Basingstoke, UK and New York: Palgrave Macmillan, pp. 54–62.

Beck, U. and Beck-Gernsheim, E. (2002) *Individualization: Institutionalised Individualism and its Social and Political Consequences*. London, Thousand Oaks and New Delhi: Sage Publications.

Berger, J. (2007) *Hold Everything Dear: Dispatches on Survival and Resistance*. London and New York: Verso.

—(2005) *Here Is Where We Are*. London: Bloomsbury Publishing Plc.

—(2001) *The Shape of a Pocket*. London: Bloomsbury.

Bergsten, C. F. (2009) The dollar and the deficits: how Washington can prevent the next crisis. *Foreign Affairs*, 88, 6 (November/December), pp. 20–38.

Berlin, I. (1996) The sense of reality, in Berlin, I. *The Sense of reality: Studies in Ideas and their History*. (ed. H. Hardy). London: Pimlico/Random House, pp. 1–39.

Blight, D., Davis, D. and Olsen, A. (2000) The globalization of higher education, in P. Scott (ed.) *Higher Education Re-formed*. London and New York: Falmer Press, pp. 95–113.

Bok, D. (2010) *The Politics of Happiness: What Governments Can Learn from the New Research on Well-Being*. Princeton: Princeton University Press.

—(2003) *Universities in the Marketplace: The Commercialization of Higher Education*. Princeton: Princeton University Press.

Brecht, B. (1966) *Parables for the Theatre: Two Plays by Bertolt Brecht* (The Good Woman of Setzuan and the Chalk Circle). (Revised English Versions by Eric Bentley) Harmondsworth: Penguin Books.

Brennan, T. (2001) Cosmopolitanism and internationalism, *New Left Review* (Second Series), 7 (January/February), pp. 75–84.

Cabrera, L. (2004) *Political Theory of Global Justice: a Cosmopolitan Case for the World State*. Abingdon, England and New York: Routledge/Taylor and Francis Group.

Calhoun, C. (2002) The class consciousness of the frequent travellers: towards a critique of actual existing cosmopolitanism, in S. Vertovec and R. Cohen (eds), *Conceiving Cosmopolitanism: Theory, Context and Practice*. Oxford: Oxford University Press, pp. 86–109.

—(1995) *Critical Social Theory: Culture, History, and the Challenge of Difference*. Oxford, UK and Cambridge, USA: Blackwell. (Chapter 7: 'The politics of identity and recognition', pp. 193–230).

Cassirer, E. (1955) *The Philosophy of Symbolic Forms. Volume Two: Mythical Thought*. (Trans. R. Manheim) New Haven and London: Yale University Press.

Cavafy, C. P. (2008) The city, in *Selected Poems*. (Trans. A. Sharon) London: Penguin Books, p. 25.

Cohan, W. D. (2009) *House of Cards: The Tale of Hubris and Wretched Excess on Wall Street*. New York: Doubleday.

Cohen, R. (1997) *Global Diaspora: An Introduction*. London: University College London Press.

Coleridge, S. T. (1965) *Biographia Literaria or Biographical Sketches Of My Literary Life and Opinions.* (Ed. G. Watson) London: Dent/ New York: Dutton.

Collingwood, R. G. (1937) *An Autobiography.* Oxford: Oxford University Press.

Collini, S. (2009) Impact on humanities: researchers must take a stand now or be judged and rewarded as salesmen, *The Times Literary Supplement*, 5563 (November 13), pp. 18–19.

—(2003) HiEdBiz: the business of higher education, *London Review of Books*, 25, 21 (6 November), pp. 3–9.

—(1993) Introduction to C. P. Snow's *The Two Cultures.* Cambridge, New York and Melbourne: Canto/Cambridge University Press.

Consodine, M. (2006) Theorizing the university as a cultural system: distinctions, identities, emergencies, *Educational Theory*, 56, 3, pp. 255–270.

Corrigan, P. (1992) The politics of Access courses in the 1990s, *Journal of Access Studies*, 7, 1, pp. 19–32.

Costanza, R., et al. (2008) An integrative approach to quality of life measurement, research, and policy, *Surveys and Perspectives Integrating Environment and Society* (SAPIENS), 1, 1. http://sapiens.revues.org/index169.html

Curran, R. C. (2000) *Aristotle on the Necessity of Public Education.* New York and Oxford: Rowman and Littlefield Publishers, Inc.

Dahrendorf, R. (1994) The changing quality of citizenship, in B. van Steenbergen (ed.)*The Condition of Citizenship.* London, Thousand Oaks, New Delhi: Sage Publications.

Darwin, C. (2009) *On the Origin of the Species: By Means of Natural Selection or the Preservation of Favoured Races in the Struggle for Life.* (Ed. W. Bynum) London: Penguin Books.

Davis, M. (2010) Who will build the Ark? *New Left Review* Second Series), 61 (January/February), pp. 29–46.

del Castillo (2009) *Rebuilding War-Torn States: The Challenge of Post-conflict Economic Reconstruction.* Oxford: Oxford University Press.

Derrida, J. (2001) *On Cosmopolitanism and Forgiveness.* (Trans. M. Dooley and M. Hughes) London and New York: Routledge/Taylor and Francis Group.

Dillon, J. T. (1994) The questions of deliberation, in J. T. Dillon (ed.) *Deliberation in Education and Society.* Norwood, NJ: Ablex, pp. 3–24.

Dunn, J. (2001) *The Cunning of Unreason: Making Sense of Politics.* London: HarperCollins Publishers.

Dunn, J. (ed.) (1992) *Democracy: the Unfinished Journey.* Oxford: Oxford University Press.

Dunne, J. (1997) *Back to the Rough Ground: Practical Judgement and the Lure of Technique.* Indiana: University of Notre Dame Press.

Dworkin, R. (1977) *Taking Rights Seriously.* London: Duckworth.

Eliot, T. S. (1969) *The Complete Poems and Plays of T.S. Eliot.* London: Faber and Faber.

Engel, J. A. (ed.) (2009) *The Fall of the Berlin Wall: The Revolutionary Legacy of 1989.* Oxford: Oxford University Press.

Engel, M. (2000) *The Struggle for the Control of Public Education: Market Ideology vs. Democratic Values.* Philadelphia: Temple University Press.

Fraser, N. (1997) *Justice Interruptus: Critical Reflections on the 'Postcolonialist' Condition.* Cambridge: Polity Press.

Gadamer, H-G. (2004) *Truth and Method.* (Second Revised Edition) London and New York: Continuum.

—(1977) *Philosophical Hermeneutics.* (Trans. and edited by D. E. Linge) Berkeley, Los Angeles and London: University of California Press.

Gamble, A. (2000) *Politics and Fate.* Cambridge: Polity.

Garton Ash, T. (2009a) 1989! *The New York Review of Books,* LVI, 17 (November 15–18), pp. 4–8.

—(2009b) Velvet revolution: the prospects, *The New York Review of Books,* LVI, 19 (December 3–16), pp. 20–23.

Genelot, D. (1994) The complex world of deliberation, in J. T. Dillon (ed.) *Deliberation in Education and Society.* Norwood, NJ: Ablex., pp. 81–98.

Giddens, A. (1993) *The Transformation of Intimacy: Sexuality, Love and Eroticism in Modern Societies.* Cambridge: Polity Press.

Giles, C. (2008) The vision thing, *Financial Times* (26 November).

Gorbachev, M. (2009) The Berlin wall had to fall, but today's world is no fairer, *The Guardian* (31 October), p. 35.

Gowan, P. (2009) The ways of the world (Interview with M. Newman and M. Bojcun) *New Left Review* (Second Series), 59 (September/October), pp. 51–70.

—(2001) Neoliberal cosmopolitanism, *New Left Review* (Second Series), 11 (September/October), pp. 79–93.

Gray, J. (2002) *False Dawn: The Delusion of Global Capitalism.* (2nd Edition) London: Granta Books.

Gutmann, A. (1987) *Democratic Education.* Princeton: Princeton University Press.

Gutmann, A. and Thompson, D. (1996) *Democracy and Disagreement.* Cambridge, MA and London: The Belknap Press of Harvard University Press.

Habermas, J. (1994) Citizenship and national identity, in B. van Steenbergen (ed.)*The Condition of Citizenship.* London, Thousand Oaks, New Delhi: Sage Publications.

Hall, J. A. (1995) In search of civil society, in J. A. Hall (ed.) *Civil Society: Theory, History, Comparison.* Cambridge: Polity Press, pp. 1–31.

Harris, J. (2009) Why public schools are likely to rule in 2010, *The Guardian* (7 November 2009), p. 14.

Harris, S. (2007) *The Governance of Education: How Neo-liberalism is Transforming Policy and Practice.* London and New York: Continuum.

Hattersley, R. (2004) Education and the good society (1), in F. Inglis (ed.) *Education and the Good Society.* Basingstoke, UK and New York: Palgrave Macmillan, pp. 12–22.

Heaney, S. (2006) *District and Circle.* London: Faber and Faber.

Heisenberg, W. (2000) *Physics and Philosophy: The Revolution in Modern Science.* London: Penguin Books

Hills, J. and others (2010) *An Anatomy of Economic Inequality in the UK: Report of the National Equality Panel.* (CASE Report 60) London: Government Equalities Office/CASE The London School of Economics and Political Science (January).

Hobsbawm, E. (2010) Interview: worlds distempers, *New Left Review* (Second Series), 61 (January/February), pp. 133–150.

—(2009) Socialism has failed. Now capitalism is bankrupt. So what comes next? *The Guardian* (10 April), p. 33.

Hoggart, R. (1982) *An English Temper: Essays on Education, Culture and Communications.* London: Chatto and Windus.

Holmes, R. (2008) *The Age of Wonder: How the Romantic Generation Discovered the Beauty and Terror of Science.* London: HarperPress.

—(1998) *Coleridge: Early Visions.* London: HaperCollins Publishers.

Honneth, A. (1995) *The Struggle for Recognition: The Moral Grammar of Social Conflicts.* (Trans. J. Anderson) Cambridge: Polity Press.

—(1991) *The Critique of Power: Reflective Stages in a Critical Social Theory.* (Trans. K. Baynes) Cambridge, MA and London: The MIT Press.

Hopkins, G. M. (1970) *The Poems of Gerard Manley Hopkins* (4th edn). (Ed. W. H. Gardner and N. H. Mackenzie) London, New York and Toronto: Oxford University Press.

Inglis, F. (2004) Education and the good society (2), in F. Inglis (ed.) *Education and the Good Society.* Basingstoke, UK and New York: Palgrave Macmillan, pp. 23–41.

Inglis, F. and Aers, L. (2008) *Key Concepts in Education.* London: Sage.

Insley, C. (2010) Letters and emails, *The Guardian* (15 January), p. 43.

Jack, I. (2009) *The Country Formerly Known as Great Britain: Writings 1989–2009.* London: Jonathan Cape.

Josipovici, G. (2010) What are universities for? (Letters to the Editor) *The Times Literary Supplement* 5571 (January 8), p. 6.

Judt, T. (2009/2010) What is living and what is dead in social democracy? *The New York Review of Books,* LVI, 20 (December 17 2009–January 13 2010), pp. 86–96.

Kerr, C. (2001) *The Uses of the University* (5th edn). Cambridge, MA and London: Harvard University Press.

Khan, I. with Petrasek, D. (2009) *The Unheard Truth: Poverty and Human Rights.* New York: W.W. Norton and Co.

King, M. (2008) Speech to the CBI, Institute of Directors, Chamber of Commerce and Yorkshire Forward, at the royal Armouries, Leeds (21 October).

Lanchester, J. (2010) *Whoops! Why Everyone Owes Everyone and No One Can Pay.* London: Allen Lane/Penguin Books.

Lingard, B. (2008) Pedagogies of indifference: research, policy and practice, in Lingard, B., Nixon, J. and Ranson, S. (eds) *Transforming Learning in Schools and Communities: The Remaking of Education for a Cosmopolitan Society.* London and New York: Continuum, pp. 209–235.

Macfarlane, B. (2007) Beyond performance in teaching excellence, in A. Skelton (ed.) *International Perspectives on Teaching Excellence in Higher Education: Improving Knowledge and Practice.* London and New York: Routledge/Taylor and Francis Group.

—(2004) *Teaching with Integrity: The Ethics of Higher Education Practice.* London: RoutledgeFalmer.

MacIntyre, A. (1999) *Dependent Rational Animals: Why Human Beings Need the Virtues.* London: Duckworth.

—(1985) *After Virtue: A Study in Moral Theory* (2nd edn). London: Duckworth.

Madano Partnership (2009) *The Class of 2010.* London: Madono Partnership.

Madrick, J. (2009) *The Case for Big Government.* Princeton and Oxford: Princeton University Press.

McDonald, L. G. with Robinson, P. (2009) *A Colossal Failure of Common Sense: the Inside Story of the Collapse of Lehman Brothers.* London: Crown Business.

McKibbin, R. (2010) Good for business, *London Review of Books*, 32, 4 (25 February), pp. 9–10.

—(2006) The destruction of the public sphere, *London Review of Books*, 28, 1 (5 January), pp. 3–6.

Mender, D. (2007) Decentering the subject of physics, *NeuroQuantology*, 5, 1, pp. 175–181.

Monbiot, G. (2001) *Captive State: The Corporate Takeover of Britain.* London: Pan (First published 2000).

Mouffe, C. (1993) *The Return of the Political.* London and New York: Verso.

Musil, R. (1997) *The Man Without Qualities.* (Trans. S. Wilkins) London: Picador.

Nixon, J. (2009a) Education and the public good, in S. Gewirtz, P. Mahoney, I. Hextall and A. Cribb (eds) *Changing Teacher Professionalism: International Trends, Challenges and Ways Forward.* Abingdon and New York: Routledge, pp. 194–203.

—(2009b) The conditions for inter-professional learning: the centrality of relationship, in C. Forbes and C. Watson (eds) *Service Integration in Schools: Research and Policy Discourses, Practices and Future Prospects.* Rotterdam/Taipei: Sense Publishers.

—(2008a) *Towards the Virtuous University: The Moral Bases of Academic Practice.* New York and London: Routledge/Taylor and Francis Group.

—(2008b) Relationships of virtue: justice as practice, in B. Lingard, J. Nixon, and S. Ranson (eds) *Transforming Learning in Schools and Communities: the Remaking of Education for a Cosmopolitan Society.* London and New York: Continuum, pp. 117–133.

—(2007) Excellence and the good society, in A. Skelton (ed.) *International Perspectives on Teaching Excellence in Higher Education: Improving Knowledge and Practice.* London and New York: Routledge/Taylor and Francis Group.

—(2006) Towards a hermeneutics of hope: the legacy of Edward W. Said, *Discourse: Studies in the Cultural politics of Education*, 27, 3, pp. 341–356.

—(2004) Learning the language of deliberative democracy, in M. Walker and J. Nixon (eds) *Reclaiming Universities from a Runaway World.* Maidenhead, England: SRHE/Open University Press, pp. 114–127.

—(1999) Teachers, writers, professionals. Is there anybody out there? *British Journal of Sociology of Education*, 20, 2, pp. 207–221.

Nixon, J. and Wellington, J. (2005) 'Good books': is there a future for academic writing within the educational publishing industry? *British Journal of Sociology of Education*, 26, 1, pp. 91–103.

Nussbaum, M. C. (2001) *Upheavals of Thought: The Intelligence of Emotions.* Cambridge: Cambridge University Press.

—(2000) *Women and Human Development: The Capabilities Approach*, Cambridge: Cambridge University Press.

—(1997) *Cultivating Humanity: A Classical Defence of Reform in Liberal Education.* Cambridge, MA and London: Harvard University Press.

—(1995) *Poetic Justice: The Literary Imagination and Public Life.* (The Alexander Rosenthall lectures Northwestern University Law School) Boston: Beacon Press.

Nussbaum, M. C. and Glover, J. (1995) *Women, Culture and Development: A Study of Human Capabilities.* Oxford: Oxford University Press.

Nussbaum, M. (1986) *The Fragility of Goodness: Luck and Ethics in Greek Tragedy and Philosophy.* Cambridge: Cambridge University Press.

Nussbaum, M. C. and Sen, A. (eds) (1993) *The Quality of Life.* A study prepared for the World Institute for Development Economics Research (WIDER) of the United Nations University. Oxford: Clarendon Press.

Odysseos, L. (2003) On the way to global ethics? *European Journal of Political Theory,* 2, 2, pp. 183–207.

O'Hagan, A. (2008) *The Atlantic Ocean: Essays on Britain and America.* London: Faber and Faber.

Pahl, R. (1995) *After Success: 'Fin-de-Siècle' Anxiety and Identity.* Cambridge: Polity Press.

Patel, R. (2009) *The Value of Nothing: How to Reshape Market Society and Redefine Democracy.* London: Portobello Books.

Peck, J. and Tickle, A. (2002) Neoliberalizing space, *Antipode,* 34, pp. 380–404.

Phillips, A. (1995) *The Politics of Presence.* Oxford: Oxford University Press.

—(1993) *Democracy and Difference.* Cambridge: Polity Press.

Pleshakov, C. (2009) *There Is No freedom Without Bread! 1989 and the Civil War that Brought Down Communism.* Los Angeles: Farrar, Straus and Giroux.

Politkovskaya, A. (2010) *Nothing But the Truth: Selected Dispatches.* (Trans. A. Tait) London: Harvill Secker.

Preece, J. (1999) *Combating Social Exclusion in University Adult Education.* Hampshire: Ashgate Publishing.

Ranson, S. (2008) Re-constructing education governance for cosmopolitan society, in Lingard, B., Nixon, J. and Ranson, S. (eds) *Transforming Learning in Schools and Communities: the Remaking of Education for a Cosmopolitan Society.* London and New York: Continuum, pp. 184–206.

Ranson, S. and Stewart, J. (1994) *Management for the Public Domain: Enabling the Learning Society.* Houndmills and London: Macmillan Press Ltd.

Rawls, J. (1971) *A Theory of Justice.* Cambridge, MA: Harvard University Press.

Ray, L. (2007) *Globalization and Everyday Life.* London: Routledge.

Raz, J. (1994) Multiculturalism: a liberal perspective, *Dissent,* Winter 67–79.

Readings, B. (1996) *The University in Ruins.* Cambridge, MA and London: Harvard University Press.

Reid, I. (1996) *Higher Education or Education for Hire? Language and Values in Australian Universities.* Rockhampton, Queensland: Central Queensland University Press.

Ricoeur, P. (2005) *The Course of Recognition.* (Trans. D. Pellaur) Cambridge, MA and London: Harvard University Press.

—(1994) *Oneself as Another*. (Trans K. Blamey) Chicago and London: The University of Chicago Press.

Rizvi, F. (2009) Towards cosmopolitan learning, *Discourse: Studies in Cultural Politics in Education*, 30, 3 (September), pp. 253–268.

—(2008) Education and its cosmopolitan possibilities, in B. Lingard, J. Nixon and S. Ranson (eds) *Transforming Learning in Schools and Communities: the Remaking of Education for a Cosmopolitan Society*. London and New York: Continuum, pp. 101–116.

Rizvi, F. and Lingard, B. (2006) Edward Said and the cultural politics of education, *Discourse: Studies in the Cultural politics of Education*, 27, 3, pp. 293–308.

Rorty, R. (1989) *Contingency, Irony and Solidarity*. Cambridge: Cambridge University Press.

Ross, A. (2003) Higher education and social access: inclusion for the masses? in L. Archer, M. Hutchings, and A. Ross with C. Leathwood, R. Gilchrist and D. Phillips, *Higher Education and Social Class: Issues of Exclusion and Inclusion*. London and New York: RoutledgeFalmer, pp. 45–74.

Ruse, M. (2001) *The Evolution Wars: A Guide to the Debates*. New Brunswick, NJ: Rutgers University Press

Said, E. W. (2004) *Humanism and Democratic Criticism*. New York: Columbia University Press.

—(2003) *Orientalism*. London: Penguin Books.

—(1993) *Culture and Imperialism*. London: Chatto and Windus.

Scanlon, T. M. (2000) *What We Owe To Each Other*. Cambridge, MA, and London: The Belknap Press of Harvard University Press.

Scott, P. (2004) The transformation of the idea of a university, in F. Inglis (ed.) *Education and the Good Society*. Basingstoke, UK and New York: Palgrave Macmillan, pp. 88–105.

Sebestyen, V. (2009) *Revolution 1989: The Fall of the Soviet Empire*. London: Orion.

Seddon, T. (2008) Remaking civic formation: transforming politics and the cosmopolitan school, in B. Lingard, J. Nixon and S. Ranson (eds) *Transforming Learning in Schools and Communities: the Remaking of Education for a Cosmopolitan Society*. London and New York: Continuum International Publishing Group, pp. 152–169.

Sen, A. (2009) *The Idea of Justice*. London: Allen Lane Penguin Books.

—(2007) *Identity and Violence: the Illusion of Violence*. London: Penguin Books.

—(1999) *Development as Freedom*. Oxford: Oxford University Press.

—(1993) Capability and well-being, in M. C. Nussbaum and A. Sen (eds) *The Quality of Life*. A study prepared for the World Institute for Development Economics Research (WIDER) of the United Nations University. Oxford: Clarendon Press.

Sennett, R. (2008) *The Craftsman*. London: Allen Lane/Penguin Books.

—(2006) *The Culture of the New Capitalism*. New Haven and London: Yale University Press.

—(1999) *The Corrosion of Character: The Personal Consequences of Work in the New Capitalism*. New York and London: W.W. Norton and Company.

—(1977) *The Fall of Public Man*. Cambridge: Cambridge University Press.

Shumar, W. (1997) *College for Sale: A Critique of the Commodification of Higher Education.* Washington, DC: The Falmer Press.

Skidelsky, R. (2009) *Keynes: The Return of the Master.* London: Allen Lane Penguin Books.

Skinner, Q. (2002) *Visions of Politics Volume 1: Regarding Method.* Cambridge: Cambridge University Press.

Slaughter, S. and Leslie, L. L. (1997) *Academic Capitalism: Politics, Policies, and the Entrepreneurial University.* Baltimore: John Hopkins University Press.

Stein, D. G. (ed.) (2004) *Buying in or Selling Out? The Commercialization of the American Research University.* New Brunswick, NJ: Rutgers University Press.

Stiglitz, J. (2010) *Freefall: Free Markets and the Sinking of the Global Economy.* London: Allen Lane/Penguin Books.

—(2006) Making globalisation work. http://www.guardian.co.uk (7 September).

—(2002) *Globalization and its Discontents.* London: Penguin Books.

—(2001) *Information and the Change in the Paradigm in Economics* (Nobel Prize Lecture) New York: Columbia Business School, Columbia University (8 December).

Su, F. (ed.) (2011) *Chinese Learning Journeys: Chasing the Dream.* Stoke on Trent: Trentham.

—(2010) *Transformations through Learning: the Experience of Mainland Chinese Undergraduate Students in an English University.* PhD Thesis, the University of Liverpool, UK. Thesis available in British Library Electronic Theses Online System (ETHOS) [on-line] at http://ethos.bl.uk

Sutton Trust (2008) *University Admissions by Individual Schools.* London: The Sutton Trust (February).

—(2006) *The Educational Backgrounds of Leading Journalists.* London: The Sutton Trust (June).

—(2005a) *The Educational Background of Members of the House of Commons and House of Lords.* London: The Sutton Trust (December).

—(2005b) *Sutton Trust Briefing Note: The Educational Backgrounds of The UKs Top Solicitors, Barristers and Judges.* London: The Sutton Trust (June).

—(2004) *The Missing 3000: State School Students Under-represented at Leading Universities.* London: The Sutton Trust (August).

Taylor, C. (2007) *A Secular Age.* Cambridge, MA and London: The Belknap Press of Harvard University Press.

—(1994) The politics of recognition, in A. Gutman (ed.) *Multiculturalism: Examining the Politics of Recognition* (2nd edn). Princeton: Princeton University Press, pp. 25–73. (Lecture inaugurating the founding of Princeton's University's Center for Human Values, 1990. First published by Princeton University Press, 1992.)

Taylor, R. (2000) Continuing education practice, lifelong learning and the construction of an accessible higher education in the United Kingdom, *Journal of Widening Participation and Lifelong Learning*, 2, 3, pp. 14–22.

Thomas, L. (2002) Student retention in higher education: the role of institutional habitus, *Journal of Education Policy*, 17, 4, pp. 423–442.

Thomas, L. and Quinn, J. (2007) *First Generation Entry into Higher Education: An International Study.* Maidenhead: SRHE/Open University Press

Todorov, T. (2002) *Imperfect Garden: the Legacy of Humanism.* (Trans. C. Cosman) Princeton and Oxford: Princeton University Press.

—(1995) *La Vie Commune: essai d'anthropologie generale.* Paris: Editions du Seuil.

Touraine, A. (2000) *Can We Live Together? Equality and Difference.* (Trans. D. Macey) Cambridge: Polity Press.

Toynbee, P. and Walker, D. (2009) *Unjust Rewards: Ending the Greed that is Bankrupting Britain.* London: Granta Books.

Trilling, L. (1951) *The Liberal Imagination: Essays on Literature and Society.* London: Martin Secker and Warburg.

University of Aberdeen (2009) *Curriculum Reform. The Final Report of the Curriculum Commission.* Aberdeen: University of Aberdeen.

Universities UK (2009) *Patterns of Higher Education Institutions in the UK: Ninth Report.* London: Universities UK (September)

Villa, D. (2001) *Socratic Citizenship.* Princeton and Oxford: Princeton University Press.

Walker, M. (2008) Capability formation and education, in B. Lingard, J. Nixon and S. Ranson (eds) *Transforming Learning in Schools and Communities: the Remaking of Education for a Cosmopolitan Society.* London and New York: Continuum International Publishing Group.

—(2006) *Higher Education Pedagogies: The Capabilities Approach.* Buckingham: SRHE/Open University Press.

—(2004) Pedagogies of beginning, in M. Walker and J. Nixon (eds) *Reclaiming Universities from a Runaway World.* Maidenhead, England: SRHE/Open University Press, pp. 131–146.

—(2003) Framing social justice in education: what does the 'capabilities' approach offer? *British Journal of Educational Studies,* 51, 2, pp. 168–187.

—(2001) *Reconstructing Professionalism in University Teaching: Teachers and Learners in Action.* Buckingham: SRHE/Open University Press.

Walsh, W. (1959) *The Use of Imagination: Educational Thought and the Literary Mind.* London: Chatto and Windus.

Warhurst, C. (2001) Using debates in developing students' critical thinking, in M. Walker (ed.) *Reconstructing Professionalism in University Teaching: Teachers and Learners in Action.* Buckingham: SRHE/Open University Press, pp. 81–104.

Westwood, S. (2002) Complex choreography: politics and regimes of recognition, in S. Lash and M. Featherstone (eds) *Recognition and Difference: Politics, Identity and Multiculture.* London, Thousand Oaks and New Delhi: Sage Publications.

Wesker, A. (1960) *The Wesker Trilogy: Chicken Soup with Barley, Roots, I'm Talking about Jerusalem.* London: Jonathan Cape.

Wilkinson, R. and Pickett, K. (2010) Thatcher's bitter bequest, *The Guardian* (30 January), p. 36.

Wilkinson, R. and Pickett, K. (2009) *The Spirit Level: Why More Equal Societies Almost Always Do Better.* London: Allen Lane.

Williams, B. (2002) *Truth and Truthfulness: An Essay in Genealogy.* Princeton and Oxford: Princeton University Press.

—(1993) *Shame and Necessity.* Berkeley, Los Angeles, London: University of California Press.

Williams, G. L. (1995) The 'marketization' of higher education: reforms and potentials in higher education finance, in D. D. Dill and B. Sporn (eds) *Emerging Patterns of Social Demand and University Reform: Through a Glass Darkly*. Oxford, New York and Tokyo: Pergamon for the International Association of Universities Press.

Williams, R. (1989) Culture is ordinary, in R. Williams *Resources of Hope: Culture, Democracy, Socialism*. (Ed. R. Gable) London and New York: Verso.

—(1958) *Culture and Society 1780–1950*. London: Chatto and Windus.

Williams, R. and Shepherd, J. (2009) Thousands of overseas students unable to enter UK, *guardian.co.uk* (14 October)

Wilson, E. (2007) *The Death of Socrates: Hero, Villain, Chatterbox, Saint*. London: Profile Books.

Wordsworth, W. (1960) *Wordsworth: The Prelude or Growth of a Poet's Mind* (Text of 1805). (Ed. E. De Selincourt) London, New York and Toronto: Oxford University Press.

Wordsworth, W. and Coleridge, S. T. (2005) *Wordsworth and Coleridge: Lyrical Ballads*. (R. L. Brett and A. R. Jones) London and New York: Routledge.

Wright, E. O. (2009) Understanding class: towards an integrated analytical approach, *New Left Review* (Second Series), 60 (November/December), pp. 101–116.

Young, I. M. (2000) *Inclusion and Democracy*. Oxford: Oxford University Press.

—(1997) Unruly categories: a critique of Nancy Fraser's dual systems theory, *New Left Review*, 222, pp. 147–160.

Young, M. F. D. (2008) *Bringing Knowledge Back In: From Social Constructivism to Social Realism in the Sociology of Education*. London and New York: Routledge/Taylor and Francis Group

Zemsky, R. (2009) *Making Reform Work: the Case for Transforming American Higher Education*. New Brunswick, NJ: Rutgers University Press.

Index

CPSIA information can be obtained
at www.ICGtesting.com
Printed in the USA
LVHW080234081020
668291LV00006B/303